DA

05-9-04

GAYLORD   PRINTED IN U.S.A.

"Geography is a science of space;
history is an art of time."
Salvador de Madaríaga

VISIONS OF GLORY

Texans on the

Southwestern Frontier

by

STEPHEN B. OATES

UNIVERSITY OF OKLAHOMA PRESS : NORMAN

By Stephen B. Oates

Confederate Cavalry West of the River (Austin, 1961)
Rip Ford's Texas (Austin, 1963)
The Republic of Texas (Palo Alto, 1968)
Visions of Glory: Texans on the Southwestern Frontier (Norman, 1970)

International Standard Book Number: 0–8061–0898–3

Library of Congress Card Number: 77–108791

Copyright 1970 by the University of Oklahoma Press, Publishing Division of the University. Composed and printed at Norman, Oklahoma, U.S.A., by the University of Oklahoma Press. First edition.

For Charles C. Alexander

Preface

Visions of Glory is a collection of my own narrative pieces,
ones that attempt to illuminate certain episodes in the evolution of Texas from a rough and rowdy frontier region
to an industrial, Space-Age society. The volume is not, and
does not purport to be, a definitive history of Texas or of
the various frontier phases through which Texas and the
Southwest have passed since the days of the Republic. Nor
does the book claim to make an argument, to develop a
closely reasoned thesis such as might be found in a book-
length essay. Rather, it is an anthology of related accounts
which have a certain thematic unity —all of them deal with
aspects of the Texan frontier, from the imperial designs of
Lamar and Houston down to NASA's historic move to Texas
in 1961—and all have a special interrelation of time and
setting that enables one to read them more or less as con-
nected episodes.

The five narratives that make up Part One enjoy a special
unity, because they are concerned primarily with military
matters (matters with which Texans themselves were preoccupied from the Texas Revolution through the Civil War)

and because they try to suggest certain traits of the American frontier character as they found expression in Texas in such events as the Snively Expedition, the exploits of the Texas Rangers in the Mexican War and on the Mexican border, and the Civil War in the Southwest. The last two chapters of the volume depart from the martial themes of the previous narratives, in part because Texans, by circumstance and by necessity, turned away from military adventures after the Civil War and increasingly concerned themselves with economic enterprise. They did so with such ambition, such improvisation, and such uninhibited gusto that in time they came to personify, in a special though frequently maligned way, the materialistic, go-for-broke entrepreneur of modern industrial America. Yet, even in the middle of the twentieth century, Texas remains a frontier community, not the brawling, hell-for-leather region it was at the time of the Snively Expedition, but an extremely complex technological frontier, one made possible by two momentous economic events—the oil boom and the space boom—events that are described in detail in the last part of this volume.

Visions of Glory has a stylistic unity too, for I wrote the accounts which it comprises not in the manner of the traditional historical essay but largely in narrative or story form. This does not mean that I made anything up or falsely colored my facts or abandoned documentation as I set about the task of writing; it simply means that when my material afforded the opportunity, I made my point through graphic scenes rather than through abstract analysis. And I did so without inventing anything *or* leaving out the footnotes.

Not that the narratives in this book are devoid of thought. They all contain reflective and expository passages. Two of them—"Texas Under the Secessionists" and "The Space

Age Comes to the Southwest"—have extensive exposition. Yet even in these accounts I tried to remember that I was writing not about "data"—faceless names and lifeless statistics—but about people who actually lived. Even in the analytical phases, then, I attempted (in the words of Aldous Huxley) "to render, in literary terms, the quality of immediate experience."

Of course, the experiences recorded in this volume are limited to a certain time and a specific place. But even so, since I have tried to recount them generally in narrative form, I hope that *Visions of Glory* transcends its regional setting to provide a glimpse of human nature in its more universal aspects: in the visions of glory and dreams of empire which Texas expansionists entertained for twenty frustrated years—in the human conflicts, the same dreams of quick fortune, the same frustration and ultimate defeat, which a column of raiders experienced out on the wind-swept Santa Fe Trail in 1843—in the fury and racial hatred generated by the much-trumpeted Texas Rangers of the Mexican War—in the story of an isolated frontier people fighting for the tragic and pitiable "lost cause" of the Confederacy—in the great Spindletop oil boom, which witnessed a recurrence of the old frontier violence even as it propelled Texas and the nation at large into a new age. Even the last account, which describes NASA's operations in Houston and suggests the virtually limitless possibilities which they portend, has comparable human themes which give the entire book a kind of dramatic continuity. For the United States space program has opened an entirely new frontier dimension in the psycho-technical complexities of our own time, when a new breed of Texas-based explorers, searching for new territory and new riches in the oceans of space beyond our world, may be inaugurating another age of exploration and empire—one in which the drama of the first Western frontier may well be played over again in the distant splendor of the stars themselves.

STEPHEN B. OATES

April, 1970
Amherst, Massachusetts

Acknowledgments

Individual portions of this book, in somewhat different form, were originally published in several quarterlies and magazines. I should like to thank the editors of the following periodicals for permission to reprint material from their pages: the *American West* for "The Hard Luck Story of the Snively Expedition" and "*Los Diablos Tejanos!*" (both of which appeared without footnotes); *True West* for "Wagon Trails West" (which was published, without documentation, as "Blazing the Trail to El Paso"); the *Southwest Review* for "Rangers on the Border" (which appeared, without footnotes, as "They Did Right Because It was Right"); the *Southwestern Historical Quarterly* for "Texas Under the Secessionists" and "The Space Age Comes to the Southwest" (which appeared as "NASA's Manned Spacecraft Center at Houston, Texas"); and *American History Illustrated* for "Roaring Spindletop" (which was printed, without documentation, as "Fabulous Spindletop"). As I set about putting these narrative accounts into book form, I revised large portions of them, especially in the opening and closing passages, added an italicized prologue to "Texas Under the Secessionists" and an introduction to Part Two, and expanded the chapters on the Texas Rangers in the Mexican War and the charting of the El Paso Trail in order to give a fuller account of these events than was possible in the originally published versions. Thus the book as it now appears is considerably different from the way it was first printed in its individual parts.

A great many people helped make this book a reality, but I should especially like to thank the Department of Research in Texas History of the University of Texas for financial assistance at the time I was working on NASA's move to Houston. In addition, I want to express my gratitude to Alwyn Barr of Texas Technological University, to James M. Grimwood of NASA's Manned Spacecraft Center in Houston, to Joe B. Frantz and Llerena Friend, both of the University of Texas, and to the Library of the University of Texas at Arlington—especially Francine Morris and Maxine Bruce—who helped in such countless indispensable ways. Finally, I owe a special debt to the late H. Bailey Carroll, an astute editor and a generous friend who gave me encouragement and financial assistance to continue my work.

STEPHEN B. OATES

Contents

PART ONE

*We were dreamers, dreaming greatly, in the
man-stifled town
We yearned beyond the sky-line where the
strange roads go down.
Came the Whisper, came the Vision, came
the Power with the Need,
Till the Soul that is not man's soul was lent
us to lead.
As the deer breaks—as the steer breaks—
from the herd where they graze,
In the faith of little children we went on our
ways.
Then the wood failed—then the food failed
—then the last water dried—
In the faith of little children we lay down and
died.*

Rudyard Kipling

I

The
Hard Luck
Story
of the
Snively
Expedition

EXAS entered 1840, her fourth year of nationhood, plagued with instabilities. Not only was her national government rife with dissension, but her treasury was empty, her commerce erratic, and her money as worthless as that of hated Mexico. Beset with such internal troubles, Texas turned away from herself, looked more and more toward the west—that symbol of man's most lavish dreams for over three centuries now—for solutions to her national difficulties. In the Texas congress, expansionists talked of conquering eastern New Mexico, which Texans claimed anyway, thereby getting control of the lucrative Santa Fe Trail. More ambitious expansionists clamored for even larger stakes: why not forge a mighty continental empire that would rival the United States, thus avenging the snub of the 1837 rejection of annexation? What these men envisioned was a Greater Texas that would include all of New Mexico, California, and several other Mexican provinces, the conquest of which would give the Republic a world outlet on two oceans and bring into her treasuries wealth beyond dreams. The expansionists swept aside all arguments that Mexico had legal title to this land. Protestant

Texas, they declared, had a God-given right to wrest from Catholic Mexico all the territory she wanted, both for her own democratic experiment and for the Anglo-Saxon race. The fact that Mexico refused to recognize Texas' independence, arguing that a state of war still existed between them, was all the excuse Texans needed to put their talk of territorial conquest into action.

Texas made her first move in 1841, when President Mirabeau B. Lamar sent an expedition out to capture Santa Fe and eastern New Mexico, and thus to divert at least part of the Santa Fe trade into Texas. But the expedition ended in disaster, as a Mexican army captured the Texan force and marched it under guard all the way to Mexico City. Texas was outraged. In retaliation, the congress passed a resolution "annexing" New Mexico, California, and all or portions of seven other Mexican provinces. But the new president, that "Dam old drunk Cherokee" Sam Houston, vetoed the resolution, remarking acidly that this was no time for a "legislative jest." Then Mexico struck back with two raids against San Antonio, the sheer audacity of which made the Texans' blood boil. When a retaliatory expedition surrendered at Mier in northern Mexico, the entire Republic howled for revenge. Houston resorted to grandiloquent tough talk, warning Mexico that if she pushed him too far, "the Texan standard of the single star, borne by the Anglo-Saxon race, shall display its bright folds in liberty's triumph on the Isthmus of Darien."[1] But all this got him was blistering criticism from Texans who were in no mood for mere tough talk: they wanted action and wanted it now.

The president himself was ready to start acting, perhaps with a series of bold strikes toward the west, when his adjutant and inspector general, a German named Jacob Snive-

---

[1] Quoted in Marquis James, *The Raven: A Biography of Sam Houston*, 322, 323. See also Llerena Friend, *Sam Houston, The Great Designer*, 82–83.

ly, approached him with a plan. Why not, Snively suggested, retaliate with a reprisal raid on Mexican caravans rumbling over the Santa Fe Trail in northern Texas? Would this not result in much booty for Houston's nearly destitute government? Would it not sate the general cry for blood which had risen since the Mier debacle, and do much to restore the general's reputation in the eyes of the Republic? Furthermore, if the expedition proved at all successful, might the raiders not push on and capture Santa Fe—as Lamar had wanted to do two years earlier—and give Texas control of all of eastern New Mexico, including the Santa Fe Trail?[2]

Houston was most impressed with this tall, bold German. Snively liked to fight and had a distinguished record: a veteran of the Texas Revolution, paymaster general, secretary of war, adjutant and inspector general now. The president wasted little time in approving of the proposed expedition. On February 16, 1843, he gave Snively a colonel's commission and ordered him to "organize and fit out an expedition for the purpose of intercepting and capturing the property of Mexican traders who may pass through the territory of the Republic." The territory Houston had in mind was the entire western portion of the Republic, which included parts of the present-day states of Oklahoma, Kansas, Colorado, and Wyoming, as well as eastern New Mexico. Snively and his raiders could keep half of whatever they captured in this area; the other half—would it be $25,000? $50,000?—would inure to Houston's government.[3] Though Snively's second Santa Fe Expedition was to be mainly one of reprisal, it might very well open the way for a larger westward thrust later on—one that would

[2] Stephen B. Oates (ed.), "Hugh F. Young's Account of the Snively Expedition as Told to John S. Ford," *Southwestern Historical Quarterly*, LXX (July, 1966), 73.

[3] M. C. Hamilton (by order of the President) to Jacob Snively, Army Papers, 1840–45 (Archives, Texas State Library, Austin).

start Texas on her much-trumpeted march toward the Pacific and toward her greater destiny as a continental power.[4]

While Houston contemplated the long-range objectives of the expedition, Snively himself went to work. He chose a place of rendezvous—Fort Johnson, located at the little settlement of Georgetown, near Coffee's Bend on the Red River —and then traveled through "the most thickly settled portions of the republic" enlisting recruits and gathering supplies.[5] By mid-April some 175 volunteers, carrying their own weapons and riding their own horses, had arrived at Fort Johnson. Most of them were young, some were unmarried, all were full of pugnacity, tired of working, and eager to make some quick money and shoot a few Mexicans. There was Hugh Franklin Young, a former buffalo hunter, restless, "straight as an Indian," as fond of fancy clothes—frock coats and silk hats—as he was of using his fists.[6] There was Eli Chandler, a troublemaker who went about Fort Johnson with a mind alert to plots. There was young Steward A. Miller, philosophic, loquacious, a compulsive diary writer destined to become the historian of the expedition. There were other recruits hardly more than boys—smooth-faced, raw as fence posts, ready to prove their manhood at the drop of an insult. Steward Miller, surveying the lot of them, noted: "They are furnished generally with a rifle, breace of pistols, & Bowie Knife. . . . That such men thus accutred, equiped, and determined should effect the object of their tour is almost beyond doubt."[7]

On April 24 Snively organized his men into three com-

---

[4] H. Bailey Carroll, "Steward A. Miller and the Snively Expedition," *Southwestern Historical Quarterly*, LIV (January, 1951), 261–64. This article also quotes liberally from a diary Miller kept while on the expedition.

[5] Oates, "Young's Account of the Expedition," *Southwestern Historical Quarterly*, LXX, 75.

[6] Hugh H. Young, *Hugh Young: A Surgeon's Autobiography*, 4–10.

[7] Carroll, "Steward A. Miller and the Snively Expedition," *Southwestern Historical Quarterly*, LIV, 269.

panies and had them choose a name for the entire outfit—
"The Battalion of Invincibles." Then, after they had elected
him commander of the expedition, he gave a victory speech
that moved everybody but Chandler to hurrahs. The next day
Commander Snively ran his men through a brisk mounted
drill on the parade grounds, pronounced them fully trained
and ready to ride, and led them out of Fort Johnson at a
jingling trot.

The column followed the Chihuahua Trail, "which passed
up the divide between the waters of the Trinity and Red
rivers," then forded the Little Washita and moved up the
Red River. On the other side of the river lay rolling brush
country that belonged to the United States. Snively had
explicit orders not to transgress on United States territory,
and he and his guide, James O. Rice, made a painstaking
effort to follow these orders to the letter.[8]

On May 5 the Texans crossed the Red River at a point
where they thought the 100th meridian to be, then struck
out to the northwest, passing the Wichita Mountains some
five days later. The land was now a flat prairie, crowded
with thick mesquite grass, which sloped away from the

[8] The eastern and northern boundaries of Texas were established by the
Adams-Oñis Treaty, ratified by Spain and the United States in 1821 and by
Mexico in 1822. The eastern boundary began at the mouth of the Sabine and
followed it up to the 32d parallel. The boundary then headed due north to
Río Roxo or Red River, following it westward "to the degree of longitude
100 west from London and 23 from Washington." The line then crossed the
Red River and ran due north to the Arkansas River, "thence following the
course of the southern bank of the Arkansas to its source, in latitude 42
north; and thence by that parallel of latitude to the South Sea. The whole
being as laid down in Melish's map of the United States." On April 25, 1838,
the United States and the Republic of Texas formally agreed to the Adams-
Oñis Treaty line as the boundary between their respective territories. William
M. Malloy (comp.), Treaties, Conventions, International Acts, Protocols, and
Agreements Between the United States and Other Powers, 1776–1909, II, 1653,
1779. The map referred to in the treaty was one that accompanied John
Melish's book, A Geographical Description of the World, Intended as an
Accompaniment to the Map of the World on Mercator's Projection. Snively's
raiders were to use that map to keep themselves within Texas territory while
they looted the Mexican trains.

mountains; in the distance they could see a herd of grazing buffalo. "What a field for the painter of rich scenery!" wrote Miller in the saddle.[9] But wood for campfires was scarce in this country, and the nights were cold and miserable.

As the raiders pushed on, fording the False Washita and Canadian rivers and heading due north, their horses began to give out with sore backs and split hooves. The column rested a day or two on the north bank of the Cimarron, in country scarcely better known than in Coronado's day. By May 25 the raiders were moving again, this time over a plain devoid of grass and water. As the wind howled out of the southwest, stirring up clouds of dust and sand that chapped their faces and parched their throats, the raiders lost what little enthusiasm they had left. "We are now at from 500 to 1,000 miles from our respective homes," Miller noted gloomily, "with but a scanty supply of provisions, in want of a proper knowledge of the country we are in, or of the distance to the place of our destination"—the Arkansas River, where the Santa Fe Trail made its crossing. "Some of us sick & borne on litters," Miller went on. "Others a foot for the want of horses, which have been lost, died, or jaded with fatigue. All suffering for want of water & one of our number having been killed, or captured by the savages" who followed the column like vultures, waiting at night, beneath a windy moon, for a chance to steal a horse or knife a sleeping sentinel.[10] At last, though, on May 27, from the top of a sand hill, the raiders sighted the Arkansas River winding lazily through a flat, windswept valley. "The whole command rushed forward," Hugh Young recalled, "and gave a

[9] Carroll, "Steward A. Miller and the Snively Expedition," *Southwestern Historical Quarterly*, LIV, 269.
[10] *Ibid.*, 273. See also Henderson Yoakum, *History of Texas from Its First Settlement in 1685 to Its Annexation to the United States in 1846*, II, 401. Yoakum's sketch of the expedition is based primarily on Miller's diary.

genuine yell before plunging into the cooling waters of the beautiful river."[11]

While the men yelled and splashed about in the water, Commander Snively sent a scout across to the other side to "ascertain the condition of things" on the nearby Santa Fe Trail.[12] The scout traveled back and forth across the trail, then reported back that although he had seen fresh wagon and hoof marks, there was no sign of Mexican trains. When Snively announced this to the men, they were bitterly disappointed; to have shot up a big Mexican caravan and taken a lot of booty would have made this a perfect day indeed. But at that moment another scout reported sighting a number of wagons near the river, perhaps a mile away. Were they Mexican? A rich train from Santa Fe? Closer inspection revealed them to be a party of Americans from Bent's Fort, a trading post on the north bank of the Arkansas in present-day Colorado, and the Texans were disappointed a second time. Colonel Snively spoke with the leader of the party, one of the Bent brothers, who thought that a Mexican caravan was now in Fort Leavenworth and would be along in eighteen or twenty days.

This new report left the raiders more dejected than before. They did not want to sit here on their haunches and wait twenty days for all that Mexican wealth to come to them. Why couldn't they cross the river, ride toward Fort Leavenworth, and intercept the train? But Snively would have none of that; his orders were to stay west of the 100th meridian, inside Texas territory, and like it or not that was what they were going to do. While the men grumbled and glared at him, the colonel moved them all downstream to a grove of trees on Crooked Creek, where they pitched camp. Snively had picked a good spot, for the raiders were now in a position to command the Cimarron branch of the Santa Fe Trail and to screen their own movements in the area.[13]

A week of inactivity passed. With nothing to do, the men grew more restless and discontented than ever, thanks in part to Eli Chandler, who moved among them spreading dissatisfaction with Colonel Snively.[14] But on June 7 their fortunes seemed to change. The lookouts thought they saw something—the Mexican train at last?—and the entire command rushed forward. But when they reached the Arkansas, the trail was empty. The men fumed and fussed, and Chandler blamed all their troubles on Snively.

The colonel quieted dissension, at least for the moment, and took his unhappy raiders into wide-open country above the point where the Cimarron branch of the trail crossed the Arkansas. Here they kept a constant watch on the horizon for signs of dust that would signal the approach of the train. Then one of the sentinels spotted something: three figures out on the prairie—and coming their way. Could they be scouts for the Mexican wagons? But luck was still against Snively's raiders, for the three men, walking boldly into the Texan camp, turned out to be Americans instead. As the raiders crowded around them, the leader introduced himself as Charles A. Warfield from Louisiana. He and his two companions had heard that Snively was out here to raid Mexican trains under authority of the Texas government. Could the colonel use three more good men? Snively, who may have heard something from Bent's party about Warfield and the sacking of some New Mexico town, seems to

---

[13] *Ibid.*, 78–80; Carroll, "Steward A. Miller and the Snively Expedition," *ibid.*, LIV, 274–75, 278.

[14] See the account of T. C. Forbes and Gilbert Ragin, *Northern Standard* (Clarksville), September 14, 1843. Forbes and Ragin, both of them survivors of the expedition, wrote to castigate Snively, calling him a coward and an incompetent. In reaction to their article, Moses Wells, R. P. Crump, Hugh F. Young, and others wrote a defense of Snively, which the *Northern Standard* carried in the issues of September 21 and 28, 1843.

have questioned all three men at some length. Finally, satisfying himself that they were all right, he let them join the command.[15]

More days of inaction and more false alarms followed. With Chandler still spreading disaffection, the men might have mutinied had not their fortunes—like the prairie wind —changed again. On June 20, as they were falling back to Crooked Creek, they sighted a body of mounted men outlined against the sky. A patrol rode out to investigate, then came galloping back yelling, *"Mexicans! Mexicans!"* In an ecstasy of nervous excitement, the raiders fell out of line and into battle formation, charging forward with all the organization of stampeding cattle. Frightened out of their wits, the Mexicans took cover in a nearby ravine. But the Texans were coming down upon them so fast, shooting so recklessly and making such an ungodly racket, that the Mexicans threw their weapons down, raised their hands, and begged to be taken prisoner. Though eighteen Mexicans had already been killed and as many others wounded, the Texans had just begun to fight. They were in no mood to take prisoners. As the Mexicans—some sixty-two of them—stared wild-eyed at the muzzles of the Texans' guns, Colonel Snively intervened. There would be no murdering of prisoners as long as he was commander of this expedition. This must have given his disgruntled troops something more to think about as they jabbed the Mexicans into line and herded them off to camp.[16]

[15] Oates, "Young's Account of the Expedition," *Southwestern Historical Quarterly*, LXX, 79; Carroll, "Steward A. Miller and the Snively Expedition," *ibid.*, LIV, 275, 278.

[16] The description of the skirmish with the Mexicans is based on Snively's report to M. C. Hamilton, June 28, 1843, Army Papers, 1840–45; Oates, "Young's Account of the Expedition," *Southwestern Historical Quarterly*, LXX, 80–81; and Miller's diary as quoted in Carroll, "Steward A. Miller and the Snively Expedition," *ibid.*, LIV, 278–79. Miller and Young both claimed that seventeen Mexicans were killed. Snively, however, put Mexican losses, out of a total engaged of ninety-eight, at eighteen killed, eighteen wounded, and sixty-two captured.

Even if Snively had shown himself a timid, overcautious man (as Chandler described him), this encounter nevertheless gave the raiders renewed hope: if Mexican troops were in the area, the rich Mexican caravan must also be nearby. It was too near sundown to go after it now, but tomorrow—tomorrow they would surely overrun it and capture—would it be ten thousand dollars worth of silks, spices, jewelry—even gold? Whatever it was to be, it was something they could all sleep on that night.

They did not sleep for long. About midnight a band of Arapahos surrounded the Texan camp on Elm Creek and came in "yelling infernally," throwing the whole command into a panic. But no sooner had the "attack" begun than it stopped. The Indians simply wanted to talk. "We were recognized as friends," Young said. "Luckily we had a full supply of buffalo meat, and were enabled to feast our red brothers in a manner they esteemed sumptuous."[17] The Indians finally departed, to the great relief of the raiders, who lay awake for the rest of the night with guns loaded and eyes on moving shadows.

All during the next week the Texans searched in vain for the promised caravan. All they found was another band of Indians—Comanches this time—who stalked the column like wolves, ambushing patrols and stragglers, and on one night suddenly burst into the Texan camp "with a big hullabaloo," stole some horses, and speared one of the pickets. Miraculously, the man lived. But after that nobody could sleep.[18]

If the nights were bad, the days were even worse, as the column wandered aimlessly up and down the river, only to fall back to Crooked Creek again. There, to add insult to misery, Colonel Snively had the gall to turn the Mexican

[17] Oates, "Young's Account of the Expedition," *Southwestern Historical Quarterly*, LXX, 81.
[18] *Ibid.*, 82.

prisoners loose. Not only did he turn them loose—he gave them mules, guns, and precious provisions too. Was Chandler right, then? Was the commander a traitor?

Aware that his men were on the verge of mutiny, Snively sent Warfield over to the United States side of the river to find out once and for all what had happened to the Mexican train. Warfield came back with the most discouraging news the Texans had heard yet: somehow he had come to the conclusion that the Mexican caravan either had gone back to Fort Leavenworth or had moved up the Pawnee Fork of the trail and would cross the Arkansas higher up, out of the Texans' reach. "This report created excitement and despondence," Young said. "We afterwards had reason to believe it false."[19]

False or not, some seventy-six of the raiders had had enough. Announcing that they were going home, they elected Chandler their commander (a move that Young and Miller, who were loyal to Snively, viewed with suspicion) and stalked out of camp. Watching them go, most of the others agreed that if the train did not come along in a few days, they too would leave. Only ten men told Snively they would stay regardless of what happened, but even the commander was losing hope now. He said they had better start hunting buffalo; the return march would be miserable in any case, and worse if they had nothing to eat.[20]

On June 29, with hunting parties scouring the area, the Texans made camp at a spot (now Ferguson Grove) on the Arkansas River, some fifty miles west of the 100th meridian as laid down on Melish's map, or about the same distance inside Texas territory as recognized by both the United

[19] Ibid. See also the account of Forbes and Ragin, Northern Standard, September 14, 1843, and that of Wells, Crump, Young, and others in ibid., September 21, 1843.

[20] Carroll, "Steward A. Miller and the Snively Expedition," Southwestern Historical Quarterly, LIV, 281; Oates, "Young's Account of the Expedition," ibid., LXX, 82–83.

States and the Texas Republic.[21] At nine o'clock the next morning, as the men were cleaning up after breakfast, they saw one of their hunters running toward the river, his arms flailing. The Texans could scarcely believe their eyes: following the hunter was a column of United States dragoons—about two hundred of them, as far as the Texans could make out—with two cannon.

The dragoons stopped a few hundred yards across the river from where the raiders stood, and prepared to make camp. At that moment the long-awaited Mexican caravan—seventy-five succulent, bulging wagons—came clattering over the trail and passed in back of the United States troops. The Texans gaped incredulously, too stunned even to curse. All at once the Americans raised a white flag. Colonel Snively, as shocked as his men, raised a white flag in return. In a moment two messengers splashed across the river. Directed to Colonel Snively, they announced that their own commander, Captain Philip St. George Cooke, wished to see the colonel in Cooke's tent. Would Snively come peacefully? He would, Snively replied, if Captain Cooke would acknowledge that this was Texas soil and would let him return without harm. "To both of these questions," Miller scribbled in his diary, "the messenger agreed."[22]

Snively then mounted and crossed over to the United States camp. Two nerve-racking hours passed. As the Texans watched intently, "wondering what it all meant," Snively emerged from Cooke's tent, mounted his horse, and headed

[21] The treaty was signed on April 25, 1838 (see note 8 above). H. Bailey Carroll, who followed the entire route of the Snively Expedition over a century later, combined the topographical information given in contemporary accounts to fix the exact location of Snively's camp "as the Ferguson Grove on the Arkansas River ten miles downstream, east of Dodge City." Thus "the Texan encampment . . . was fifty miles west of the 100th meridian and therefore that distance within the territory of the Republic." Carroll has abundant documentary evidence to support his findings. Carroll, "Steward A. Miller and the Snively Expedition," *ibid.*, LIV, 282–83.

[22] *Ibid.*, 281.

toward the ford. But Captain Cooke called him back. There was a bustle in the American camp. The dragoons saddled up. Captain Cooke led them, along with Snively and his escort, across the river and beyond a belt of timber to the edge of the prairie. Here the dragoons deployed with blood-chilling precision. In a moment the Texans were invested on three sides. The dragoons cocked their guns. Across the river the howitzers were rolled into position. The gunners lit their matches. It was going to be a massacre.

The raiders crowded together like trapped animals. But the dragoons did not fire. Slowly Colonel Snively rode back to the Texan camp. He announced that Captain Cooke had given them exactly thirty minutes to surrender unconditionally or be shot. There was a long silence. Then a few of the men protested. What right did Cooke have to order such a thing? The Texans were in their own territory, had broken no laws, violated no treaties, killed no Americans, stolen no property—until a few hours ago they had not even *seen* any property—so how, by what human or legal right, could Captain Cooke demand their surrender? Could the colonel not try to reason with the madman? Colonel Snively rode out, but came back in a few minutes and said it was no use. A couple of belligerents were ready to fight it out, but the others, eying those menacing cannon, lost heart. Stacking their muskets (and concealing a few knives and pistols beneath their clothes), they surrendered.

More humiliation was to come. When Snively pleaded with Cooke to let the Texans keep enough muskets to defend themselves, pointing out that there were hostile Indians all along their return route, "the generous officer," Young recorded sarcastically, "permitted us to retain ten guns, with ten rounds of ammunition to each gun," and told them to leave the area at once. Cooke then led his troops back across the river to their camp. The Texans were so crushed that they could scarcely look at one another. Yes, "it was humiliating," Young wrote. But outmanned, outgunned, and outmaneuvered as they were, what else could they do?[23]

With their ten guns (plus the pistols and knives they had concealed), the raiders moved to Elm Creek the next morning, feeling more hatred for Cooke than they felt even for Santa Anna.

Their commander might well have felt the same way. Perhaps he even agreed with some of his men that "the dastard Cooke"—that was the mildest name they called him—had been bribed by the Mexicans to disarm the Texan force. Of course, it was possible that the captain had made a mistake, thinking he was still in United States territory when he confronted the raiders. But what bothered Snively—and would bother many other Texans for years—was how Cooke could have marched fifty miles west of the 100th meridian (as laid down on Melish's map) and still think he was on United States soil. His own maps and guides could not have been *that* inaccurate, could they?[24]

Another thing: why had the United States sent Cooke out to protect the Mexican train and to disperse the Snively

[23] Oates, "Young's Account of the Expedition," *ibid.*, LXX, 83–84. See also the account of Wells, Crump, Young, and others, *Northern Standard*, September 21, 1843.

[24] Although the meridian had not been marked by surveys or astronomical reckonings, Cooke should have known that he was west of the 100th meridian and so inside Texas territory, since he was using Melish's map just as Snively was doing. Later, in 1896, the United States Supreme Court ruled that the 100th meridian as given on this map was inaccurate and that modern surveys had established the true 100th meridian as running between ranges 24 and 25 east of present-day Dodge City, Kansas. Thus Snively's camp on the Ferguson Grove was about ten miles east of the true 100th meridian, but, as Carroll points out, "certainly Snively in 1843 had every justification for his belief that he was within Texan territory," since both nations then were using the meridian on Melish's map. Carroll, "Steward A. Miller and the Snively Expedition," *Southwestern Historical Quarterly*, LIV, 282–83. On the other hand, Leo E. Oliva, in his *Soldiers on the Santa Fe Trail*, 46–49, argues on the basis of Cooke's own account that the Texans were camped ten miles east of the 100th meridian, "as later determined," and that therefore *they* were mistaken in thinking they were in Texan territory.

column in the first place? Doubtless, Cooke had told Snively what his orders were: to dispel any Texas land pirates he found operating on the western end of the Santa Fe Trail. He had not, however, explained why such orders had been issued and why he and his government regarded Snively's column as a band of land pirates.

What Snively could not have known was that the United States had suffered considerable national embarrassment because of two other raiding parties that had insisted that they too were operating under full authority of the Texas government. The first of these had been led by none other than Charles A. Warfield—the same Warfield who had joined Snively and his men sometime between June 7 and June 20. Warfield had been authorized by President Houston to raid Mexican trains crossing Texas-claimed territory on the Santa Fe Trail some six months before Snively, and had led a band of twenty-four men up to the Arkansas River, near the junction of the Río de las Animas. Apparently Warfield had cared nothing for boundaries or legalities, roaming United States territory at will. Then, in May, while Snively was marching toward the Arkansas, Warfield's band attacked the settlement of Mora in the extreme northeastern portion of New Mexico, killing five Mexicans, capturing eighteen, and stealing seventy-two horses. Soon afterward, a Mexican column overtook the invaders and scattered them in a hot, running fight. The remnants of Warfield's force walked to the vicinity of Bent's Fort and disbanded. Warfield himself and two of his men had wandered over the area until they came upon Snively's camp near the Arkansas.

In the meantime, Mexican authorities complained bitterly to United States officials about Warfield's invasion. The New Mexico governor, Don Manuel Armijo, even sent a force of cavalry to guard the lives and property of Mexican merchants who crossed the trail. Snively, of course, had known that Armijo had a sizable force somewhere along the trail. The Mexicans he had captured on June 20 had been a part of it. What Snively did not know was why the Mexicans were patrolling the trail in the first place.

The second "land pirate" was one John McDaniel, who had robbed and killed a well-known Albuquerque merchant near the Little Arkansas, inside the boundaries of the United States. News of the crime spread like a prairie fire, and United States lawmen soon apprehended McDaniel and his men. Hoping for clemency, McDaniel described himself as "lately from Texas" and claimed to have acted on the full authority of Houston's government. Predictably, American newspapers sensationalized the story, damning Texas for sanctioning the work of murderers and thieves. When United States authorities learned of Snively's presence on the Arkansas, they assumed that he was leading another band of cutthroats. Cooke's cavalry was forthwith dispatched to protect the Mexican caravan from Fort Leavenworth and to disarm and drive off any hostile Texans found in United States territory.[25]

Snively, though, knew nothing about McDaniel's work and perhaps nothing about Warfield's. Even if he had known, one nagging question would have remained: why had Cooke invaded Texas territory to carry out his orders? Was it really for "a monetary consideration" or simply a driving desire to interpret his orders in their broadest possible sense in order to spare his government further embarrassment? Snively himself did not know. Perhaps nobody would ever know what had prompted Cooke to do what he had done.[26]

[25] For further information on Warfield's and McDaniel's activities, see Rufus B. Sage, *Scenes in the Rocky Mountains, and the Grand Prairies*, 244; Josiah Gregg, *Commerce of the Prairies: The Journal of a Santa Fe Trader*, II, 172–73; and William C. Binkley, *The Expansionist Movement in Texas, 1836–1850*, 106–18.

[26] Carroll, arguing for the legality of the Snively Expedition, believes that since Cooke's government was an avowed neutral in the continuing war be-

But Snively had more immediate concerns than the motives of Captain Cooke. The day after the capture, Eli Chandler and his "home boys" (Miller's sardonic name for them) staggered into Snively's camp. Instead of going home, they had wandered about the Arkansas hoping to find the Mexican caravan for themselves, but they had found nothing, nothing at all. Now they were half dead from hunger and exhaustion. Would Snively have the decency to give them food and let them travel along with him? After all, the more men the colonel had, the stronger his force would be should they encounter Indians or Mexican cavalry.

Snively, a decent man, agreed to let them come along. It was a mistake. He and Chandler began quarreling immediately, and soon the entire column was rife with dissension. Twelve men deserted, crossing the Arkansas and joining Cooke's command. Most of the other raiders, goaded on by Chandler's men, blamed the futility of the expedition on the blind incompetence of their commander. Hearing that, Snively "resigned the command of the battalion, in disgust at the want of subordination of men & subalterns, indignantly breaking his sword & thrusting it to the ground."[27]

Warfield then stepped forward and offered a proposition: the Mexican caravan Captain Cooke had escorted to the Arkansas river was well inside Texas territory by now and was unprotected. They could take it easily, then hightail it for home before Cooke found out. Who would follow him? The men whispered among themselves. Sixty-two of them

tween Texas and Mexico, the captain proved himself "an out-and-out partisan on the Mexican side" by crossing into Texas territory to disarm a retaliatory force operating with full sanction of the Texas government. Carroll, "Steward A. Miller and the Snively Expedition," *Southwestern Historical Quarterly*, LIV, 283. William C. Binkley also argues for the legality of the expedition in *The Expansionist Movement in Texas*, 115–16. Captain Cooke's account of the Snively capture is in William E. Connelley (ed.), "A Journal of the Santa Fe Trail," *Mississippi Valley Historical Review*, XII, (September, 1905) 225–34.

[27] Carroll, "Steward A. Miller and the Snively Expedition," *Southwestern Historical Quarterly*, LIV, 284–85.

stepped forward. But Chandler and some forty others thought it was useless to chase any more fugitive trains and set out for home—this time in earnest. Warfield, with Snively tagging stubbornly along, led the others westward, promising them that they would soon be rich men.

On July 13 they reached the Cimarron Springs, where they found the ashes of two large campsites—one made by Mexican cavalry, the other by the big caravan. The latter was evidently the most recent, which meant that the cavalry was ahead of the train rather than behind it. The raiders were ecstatic. At last, after two months of rotten luck, providence seemed to favor them. They lined up in the road and prepared to march. To their immeasurable shock, Warfield suddenly claimed that the Mexican cavalry was in back of the Mexican train, not in front of it—he knew these treacherous Mexicans—and that they were marching into an ambush. Miller protested that all the evidence proved the contrary, but Warfield turned his mule southward. "Men," he yelled, "I am going to the interior of Texas. All wishing to go home will follow me."[28]

When Warfield started forward, it was the final blow. One by one the raiders fell in behind him, quite as though he had them in chains. Finally only ten men remained, among them Colonel Snively. After a brief consultation, they picked up their weapons, cursed their luck, and followed after the "double-dealing" Warfield.[29]

Two days later the raiders had become more dissatisfied with Warfield than they had ever been with Snively. They suspected that Young was right—that Warfield was a traitor. Consequently they "notified him of their desire to accept his resignation. It was tendered, and Col. Snively again selected to command." Snively had been exonerated, so to speak.

[28] Oates, "Young's Account of the Expedition," *ibid.*, LXX, 86.
[29] *Ibid.*

But there was to be more bad luck ahead. On the return march, Indians killed five raiders, two others got in a fight, one killing the other, and the rest, suffering from exposure and exhaustion, went the last four days with nothing to eat at all. The remnants of the "Battalion of Invincibles" dragged themselves into Bird's Fort, halfway between present-day Dallas and Fort Worth, and there disbanded on August 6, 1843. "The Santa Fe expedition," Young recorded with masterful understatement, "was a failure."[30]

When Snively reported to Houston, the president was furious about the encounter with Cooke. This was another national insult. But since Houston was already maneuvering to get Texas annexed to the United States, there was nothing he would do but make a polite protest to President Tyler. Tyler agreed to look into the matter, and several months later he called a court of inquiry to investigate Cooke's actions. The court convened at Fort Leavenworth on April 2, 1844, spent a little over three weeks reviewing the case, and concluded that Cooke had disarmed Snively's raiders not on Texas soil but "within the territory of the United States" and that he had in no way exceeded his authority.[31]

The raiders were scandalized when they learned of the court's decision, but hardly anyone else in Texas cared much one way or the other. Since the failure of the Snively Expedition, the Republic had ceased dreaming of empire. Now she looked to the United States for solutions to her manifold problems, and worked assiduously for annexation. There was considerable opposition to annexation in New England, not only because Texas was "a slave place" but also (in the words of a Massachusetts Whig) because of her "population of lawless renegade ruffian adventurers."[32]

[30] *Ibid.*, 86, 87–88. See also the account of Forbes and Ragin, *Northern Standard*, September 14, 1843.
[31] Quoted in Yoakum, *History of Texas*, II, 495n.
[32] John S. Ford, *Rip Ford's Texas* (ed. Stephen B. Oates), 45.

But American expansionists, envisioning their own continental empire, overcame such opposition, and the United States Congress offered to annex Texas by a joint resolution in February, 1845. Texas quickly met the requirements, drafting a state constitution that guaranteed a republican government. On December 29, 1845, President James K. Polk, an enthusiastic expansionist, signed the bill that annexed Texas to the United States, thereby setting in motion a spiral of accusation and counteraccusation with Mexico which would shortly plummet the two republics into war.

Neither annexation nor the war with Mexico ended the controversy over the Snively Expedition—or the hard luck of the surviving raiders. Snively himself, bitten by the gold bug, set out for California after the great gold strike of 1848. For twenty years he searched the West for gold as fruitlessly as he had looked for Mexican caravans back in 1843, only to die of an Apache arrow, near the settlement of Vulture, in 1871.[33]

In the meantime, several of the raiders petitioned the United States government, protesting the decision of the Fort Leavenworth court and demanding that they be generously compensated for the weapons which Cooke had taken from them. President Polk thought the raiders had a just claim and called on Congress to do something to settle the matter. After several delays and considerable debate, during which the actual location of the Snively capture received only passing attention, the Senate finally passed an act, approved on March 3, 1847, that gave Texas $30,000 as a compensation not only for the arms that the Snively Expedition had lost, but also for goods that a band of men from the

[33] For additional biographical data on Snively, see Biographical Information Sheet, which Senator Carl Hayden of Arizona sent to Harriet Smithers (Archives, Texas State Library, Austin) ; and John Henry Brown, *History of Texas from 1685 to 1892*, II, 287–91.

United States had stolen from the customhouse at Bryarly's Landing on the Red River. The survivors of the expedition ultimately received $18.75 apiece.[34]

Insulted by such a trifling amount, they sent another petition to the United States government demanding at least twice that much money. Texas Senator Thomas J. Rusk introduced a resolution to pay the raiders what they asked for, but the Senate voted it down. When the raiders learned of the vote, they unleashed all their pent-up frustrations on the other Senator from Texas—Sam Houston. They accused Houston of speaking out against the resolution, of telling the entire Senate that he had not authorized the Snively Expedition to march up to the Santa Fe Trail, of dropping the accusation that the column was "an organization of bandits —or words to that effect." This alleged denunciation had supposedly turned the Senate against Rusk's resolution, and Sam Houston had thus "rebuked, and defeated the just claims, of the men who had undergone privations and hardships to serve Texas at his bidding. His action in the premises is one of those anomalies not to be accounted for on any known principle of philosophy, or any rule of logic."[35]

This accusation has never been substantiated by any known evidence.[36] But while the author was doing research on the expedition in the summer of 1963, he heard that someone still living—someone, it was alleged, who had a vested interest in preserving Houston's good name—was concealing evidence which would prove that Houston had lied about his connections with the raid and had called Snively's men a band of thieves. The author is inclined to

[34] U.S., *Statutes at Large, 1847*, IX, 168; *Congressional Globe* (Washington, D.C.), January 9, 12, February 5, July 14, 1846, pp. 145, 162, 291, 1073.
[35] Oates, "Young's Account of the Expedition," *Southwestern Historical Quarterly*, LXX, 89–90.
[36] See the editor's note in *ibid.*, 90–91.

doubt this allegation, but it does indicate that some Texans, after 126 years, are still concerned with the reputation of Sam Houston as it is reflected in the story of Jacob Snively and his hard-luck raiders.

II

Los
Diablos Tejanos!

IN THE sweltering twilight of May 22, 1846, a company
of sunburned, grim-faced Texas Rangers, the advance
unit of a newly organized Texas Regiment, rode into
Fort Brown, the farthest southern outpost of Anglo-American civilization in Texas and combat headquarters of General Zachary "Old Rough and Ready" Taylor, commander
of the Army of the Río Grande. The war with Mexico over
the annexation of Texas and ultimate control of the American Southwest had officially begun only nine days ago, but
Taylor's troops had already won two decisive victories over
a demoralized Mexican army and sent it in headlong retreat
for Monterrey, some 175 miles southwest of Fort Brown.
The possibilities of crushing this army and ending the war
in northern Mexico were bright indeed, and Taylor was already moving his veterans across the river to Matamoros
when the Rangers reached Fort Brown. Captain Ben Mc-
Culloch, company commander, reported to the general that
night while the men themselves made camp and oiled their
guns, hoping to see action at once. They were not disappointed. Taylor promptly ordered McCulloch to scout the
arid land between Matamoros and Monterrey and find a

good route for his army to follow. The next morning, as the Texans crossed into Mexican territory, they broke into their celebrated "Texas Yell." At last—at long last—they could shoot Mexicans legitimately and shoot to kill.

It was not long before the rest of the Texas Regiment, under the over-all command of a convivial, boy-faced colonel named John C. "Jack" Hays, arrived at Matamoros and also started scouting for Taylor's army.[1] The general no doubt expected a great deal from Hays's outfit. The Texas Rangers were veteran Indian fighters, known for their extraordinary courage and endurance. As individual fighters they were virtually incomparable: almost no one could fire a six-shooter with more accuracy; almost no one could move quicker and use a bowie knife with more skill in close-quarter combat. But as soldiers who had to respect rank and order, these Rangers were beyond hope; they soon proved themselves so wild and tempestuous and utterly uncontrollable that even Taylor, as spirited and independent as any man, came to regard them as barbarians, as "licentious vandals."[2] For no sooner had they arrived in Mexico than they began to commit shocking atrocities. They raided villages and pillaged farms; they shot or hanged unarmed Mexican civilians. On one occasion Taylor lost his temper altogether and threatened to jail the lot of them. The occasion was a Fourth of July celebration at Reynosa in which

[1] Hays, under authority of the governor, had recruited the regiment in the late spring of 1846. Before the outfit was fully organized, Hays permitted McCulloch's and R. A. Gillespie's companies, ready for battle before the rest, to report to Taylor for special scouting services on the understanding that they would rejoin him in August. The captains of the other eight companies in Hays's regiment were C. B. Acklin, S. L. S. Ballowe, Eli Chandler (the same troublemaking Chandler who had accompanied the Snively Expedition), F. S. Early, J. Gillespie, Tom Green, C. C. Herbert, and Jerome B. McCown. U.S. War Department, Records Group No. 94 (National Archives, Washington, D.C.). See also James Kimmons Greer, *Colonel Jack Hays: Texas Frontier Leader and California Builder*, 126–29, 385n.

[2] Taylor to George T. Wood, July 7, 1846, Governors' Letters, 1846–60 (Archives, Texas State Library, Austin).

the Texans stole two horse buckets of whisky to wash down a meal of Mexican pigs and chickens which they had killed "accidentally" while firing salutes to honor the day.[3]

What could Taylor do with such men? He could not put all seven hundred of them in the guardhouse—no matter how much he might like to—because the Rangers would be indispensable as scouts once the army began the advance on Monterrey. As one of their own put it, the Rangers "were not only the eyes and ears of General Taylor's army, but its right and left arms as well."[4] Nevertheless, the general had to do something, for on August 2 he received a report that the Rangers were at it again. While encamped at Matamoros, they attended theaters, jingling spurs on their boots, rifles in their hands, Colt revolvers in their holsters, and pistols and bowie knives tucked in their belts. They not only frightened the citizenry but also picked fights with regulars in the United States Army and shot at makeshift targets in the middle of town.[5]

What, Taylor kept asking, made these men do such things? Was it simply inherent in their nature? Were they criminals? Were they mad? Or had it something to do with the wild frontier beyond the Río Grande whence they came, that land whose revolution some ten years earlier had finally led to this war which Taylor was committed to win? For Texas in 1846 was indeed a hard, cruel frontier whose soil was thin and dry, whose commerce was slight, whose Indians were belligerent and, if Tonkawas, were man-eaters—a land where pioneers, if they lived at all, lived by their own cunning and granite will. The Rangers themselves—like the

[3] S. C. Reid, Jr., *The Scouting Expeditions of McCulloch's Texas Rangers,* 53, 61.

[4] W. H. King, "The Texas Ranger Service and History of the Rangers, with Observations on Their Value as a Police Protection," in Dudley G. Wooten (ed.), *A Comprehensive History of Texas,* II, 338.

[5] John R. Kenly, *Memoirs of a Maryland Volunteer, War with Mexico in the Years 1846–7–8,* 53.

men who accompanied the Snively Expedition three years earlier—came from the fringe areas of frontier Texas, from the thickly wooded and red-hilled districts in the east, from the twisted mesquite country in the west, and the sweltering brush regions in the far south. They came from a land whose civilization was divided into little remote pockets of settlers who had gathered together out of a common fear—a fear of coming violence, a fear of the unknown. Such isolated communities had only a trace of civil organization, almost no law, and one overriding justice: revenge. Yes, vengeance was the moving spirit—a spirit of passion—by which men enforced their rights in frontier Texas. Avenge the horses which renegade Indians had stolen by moonlight; avenge those stout, red-necked women whom Comanche bands had roped and dragged through prickly pear until they were mangled beyond recognition as human; avenge the insults which a neighbor had shouted in moments of cold fury; avenge the friend who had died in the metallic blaze of some stranger's guns; and now, for the Texas Rangers fighting with Taylor, avenge the fathers and brothers, uncles and cousins, whom the Mexicans had slain at the Alamo and Goliad, at Santa Fe and Mier and the Hacienda Salado in the infamous "black bean" episode. Yes, if Taylor was looking for an answer, this was it: this persisting compulsion to avenge atrocites committed upon their people now moved the Texans to commit atrocities themselves—to hang Mexican civilians, to gun down peon farmers in the moving sand south of the river, to fire over the heads of little brown boys running barefoot through the streets of Matamoros.

Somehow, though, Taylor had to discipline them, or President Polk, who did not like the general for political reasons, might reprimand him in public for waging an uncivilized war.[6] The trouble was that the Rangers were beyond discipline, and Taylor knew it. It was impossible to control hard-boiled frontiersmen who liked to drink and swear and who were in Mexico to settle a score and were not to be bothered by rules and regulations in going about it. Except perhaps for Colonel Hays, who was mild mannered when he was not in battle, their officers had the same attitude: veteran fighters like Ben McCulloch, cold and austere in features, who had hunted bears in Tennessee before coming to Texas, and Samuel Walker, whose hatred for Mexicans was as famous as the six-shooters he carried strapped to his legs. These men had become officers not because they could give orders or click their heels but because they could outfight anyone in their commands.[7]

Because of their attitude about fighting, Taylor had some misgivings in sending the Rangers 130 miles southwest to scout the area between San Fernando and China when the army, after nearly a month of final battle preparations, at last set out for the Mexican stronghold at Monterrey. On this scout the Rangers lived up to his expectations, not only as the eyes and ears of his main column, but also as "licentious vandals" who committed further outrages. A glaring example was the time they caught a poor wretch trying to steal one of their horses and decided to show Mexicans in that region how Texans administered justice. They tied, gagged, and shot him dead, leaving the corpse in the blowing sand as they mounted and rode northwest toward Monterrey.[8]

---

[6] Taylor and Polk had been feuding since the war began. Not only were they personally antagonistic to each other, but they belonged to different political parties, too: Taylor was a Whig and Polk a Democrat. The President feared that Taylor's victories were making him uncomfortably popular in the public eye, that continued success might make him a national hero in the mold of Andrew Jackson and thus presidential potential. Polk would, therefore, take every advantage to disparage Taylor that he could find. See Otis A. Singletary, *The Mexican War*, 104–16.

[7] Walter Prescott Webb, *The Texas Rangers: A Century of Frontier Defense*, 95, 99.

[8] Reid, *Scouting Expeditions of McCulloch's Texas Rangers*, 108–109.

The Rangers overtook Taylor at Marin on September 17, and the combined force then marched through light and darkness to a group of tree-shaded springs known as the Bosque de San Domingo (the Americans called the place the Walnut Springs), about two miles northeast of Monterrey. It was here that the Texans' vandalism gave way to something even more annoying: a persistent refusal to follow orders. When McCulloch's Rangers, followed by Taylor himself and his immediate staff, made a reconnaissance the next day, the Texans kept looking at a black fort about halfway between the American camp and the city. Taylor warned them not to try anything, but the Rangers ignored him, let out an ear-splitting yell, and charged the fort without order or organization. "Like boys at play," said a regular who watched them in awe, "those fearless horsemen in a spirit of boastful rivalry, vied each other in approaching the very edge of danger. Riding singly and rapidly, they swept around the plains under the walls, each one in a wider and more perilous circle than his predecessor. Their proximity occasionally provoked the enemy's fire, but the Mexicans might as well have attempted to bring down skimming swallows as those racing dare-devils."[9]

Taylor, looking on in disbelief, at last called them back, but there was little he could do except order them back to camp. There the general prepared the whole army, 6,230 strong, for attack the next day. For better or worse, the Rangers had precipitated the crucial five-day battle for Monterrey. On Sunday, September 20, 1846, as Taylor's main columns struck the northeastern section of the city, General William J. Worth's division, led by Hays's Texans, flanked Monterrey and approached it from the northwest along the

---

[9] [Luther Giddings] *Sketches of the Campaign in Northern Mexico in Eighteen Hundred Forty-Six and Seven by an Officer of the First Ohio Volunteers*, 143.

Saltillo road.[10] With the Texans still in front, Worth's contingent flung itself against the forts that protected the rear of town; Federation Hill and Fort Salado fell on September 21, then Independence Hill and the Bishop's Palace, which McCulloch's men, shrieking like Comanches, captured almost singlehanded.

On the third day of battle, September 23, a storm broke with rolling thunder and lightning that danced across the tops of the buildings. While the rain fell and fell harder still, Hays's Rangers and light infantry drove into the city proper, shooting at enemy soldiers in windows and on roof tops, tunneling through adobe walls with crowbars and picks, sprinting through narrow streets that the rain had converted into small streams full of debris and corpses. Hand-to-hand fighting in the streets continued through the night and most of the next morning when the Ranger captains received an order from General Worth to withdraw so that Taylor's artillery could shell the city before the main attack began. Outraged, the Texans sent back a note that they had carried the lower part of the city by themselves and that they would not budge. In a few moments the bombardment commenced with the Texans still in the target area, but as if by a miracle none of them were hurt. They soon received another message to hold their positions while the commanding general and the Mexicans had a talk. By nightfall an understanding had been reached, and the Mexicans began to evacuate. Soon after, on October 2, 1846, the Rangers, whose six months' enlistments were over, set out for Texas in pairs and groups; Colonel

[10] Unless otherwise cited, the account of the Texas Rangers at Monterrey is based on the following sources and books: Hays to General J. Pinckney Henderson, September 24(?), 1846, in *The Papers of Mirabeau Buonaparte Lamar* (ed. Charles A. Gulick), IV, pt. 1, p. 139; W. J. Worth's report, September 28, 1846, 29th Cong., 2d sess., *House Exec. Doc. 4*, 102ff.; Reid, *Scouting Expeditions of McCulloch's Texas Rangers*, 153–93; John S. Ford, "Truitt at Monterey," in Ford, Memoirs (Archives, University of Texas Library, Austin), IV, 619–22; Webb, *Texas Rangers*, 102–10; and Greer, *Colonel Jack Hays*, 137–53.

Hays and staff were the last to go in mid-October, and regulars who watched them leave praised them for their extraordinary fighting abilities. "Had it not been for their unerring rifles," one volunteer remarked, "there is no doubt we would have been whipped at Monterrey."[11] Others recalled the Texans fiercely "charging on the guns which swept the slippery streets," but Colonel Hays had been heard to admit that the Mexicans "were damn poor shots or not a mother's son of us could have got them."[12]

General Taylor also grudgingly commended them for gallant action, even if they had disobeyed orders, and watched them ride off with unmitigated relief: the prospect of having seven hundred idle Texans in Monterrey now that the fighting was finished was a foreboding thought, even for "Old Rough and Ready."[13]

Taylor, however, had not seen the last of the Texas Rangers. Captain McCulloch and twenty-seven of his most pugnacious Texans returned to Mexico when they heard that Santa Anna himself was leading an army over the desert with a ringing promise to drive the "gringos" from Mexico or perish in the attempt. Taylor received the Texans cordially enough, putting them to work as scouts and couriers. On February 16, while the American army entrenched at Agua Nueva, the general sent the Texans across the desert to scout Santa Anna's position at Encarnación, about thirty-five miles south of Monterrey.[14] Beneath a sliver of moon, the Rangers slipped inside enemy lines and came finally to a low ridge overlooking the Mexican army, encamped on a

[11] T. W. Ridell to A. P. Murgotten, January 18, 1901, in the *Pioneer* (San Jose, California), February 15, 1901, as cited in Greer, *Colonel Jack Hays*, 153, 387n.

[12] Edward Bosque, *Memoirs*, 34n.

[13] Order No. 124, October 1, 1846, 30th Cong., 1st sess., *House Exec. Doc. 60*, 508; Webb, *Texas Rangers*, 110.

[14] Taylor to Adjutant General, June 8, 1847, 30th Cong., 1st sess., *House Exec. Doc. 60*, 1176.

vast plain. It was a chilling sight: tents and huts as far as the Texans could see and thousands of men and wagons moving about in the flickering shadows of orange watch fires. In a few moments a party of Rangers slid down the ridge and crawled from fire to fire counting bedrolls and cannon and occasionally knifing a careless sentinel; at last they rejoined the others on the ridge, then all the Texans rode under the noses of Mexican pickets and raced back to report. Santa Anna, they concluded, had over twenty thousand men and a far superior field position for the forthcoming battle.[15] Knowing then that he was heavily outnumbered, Taylor ordered a withdrawal from his exposed position at Agua Nueva to an almost impregnable one behind the Angostura Pass near Buena Vista where he could not be flanked. That afternoon, with blare of trumpet and tuck of drum, Santa Anna's legions attacked, but Taylor's army turned back assault after assault and at last forced the Mexicans to withdraw. Had the Rangers not been there to scout for him, Taylor might have engaged the Mexicans at Agua Nueva and gone down to defeat.[16]

As it was, Taylor had won a brilliant victory, a victory that ended the war in northern Mexico and made him popular enough in the public eye to become a serious presidential possibility. He would have thanked the Texas Rangers for their good work had they not become exasperatingly troublesome. With inactivity, they took to brawling and to committing "extensive depredations and outrages" on Mexican civilians. "The mounted men from Texas," Taylor complained, "have scarcely made one expedition without unwarrantably killing a Mexican," and they had indulged in practically every other "form of crime" as well. When their enlistments ended and they set out for home, the general

15 Reid, *Scouting Expeditions of McCulloch's Texas Rangers*, 234–35.
16 Webb, *Texas Rangers*, 113.

declared that because of the "constant recurrence of such atrocities," he urgently requested that no more Texans come to help his army.[17]

The Texans, however, were not through fighting yet. Between April and July, 1847, Jack Hays recruited a second regiment of Rangers, many of whom had already seen action with Taylor, and prepared first to serve on the Indian frontier and then, under new orders, to reinforce Taylor, whose rear echelons were under constant harassment from Mexican guerrillas.[18] The officer corps of the second regiment was made up of tough, battle-hungry captains like Alfred Truitt, Isaac Ferguson, Samuel Highsmith, Gabriel M. Armstrong, Jacob Roberts, Alfred Evans, and staff officers like Major Michael Chevaille and Adjutant John S. Ford, a tall, restless frontier doctor who would keep a record of Ranger action throughout 1847 and 1848. Many of the five hundred enlisted men were jobless adventurers and would prove more violent and uncontrollable than those of Hays's first regiment.[19]

In mid-August, 1847, the command rode to Mier, Mexico, where "our entrance caused some excitement among the Mexicans," who nursed "bitter recollections" of the battle of Mier fought here some four years earlier. As the horsemen passed through the streets, one "good looking" señora shouted to them: "I had rather see every relative I have, dead, here, before my eyes, than to see the Texans enter

[17] Taylor to Adjutant General, June 16, 1847, 30th Cong., 1st sess., *House Exec. Doc. 60*, 1178.

[18] Originally Hays had raised a second regiment to protect Taylor's supply lines between Monterrey and the Río Grande, but then word came that the general would receive no troops for less than twelve months, and several of the companies disbanded. Within weeks, however, Hays's recruiters raised enough new companies to constitute a regiment of twelve months' volunteers. On July 10, in San Antonio, the outfit was mustered into federal service for twelve months or for the duration of the war. U.S. War Department, Records Group No. 94 (National Archives, Washington, D.C.) ; W. J. Hughes, *Rebellious Ranger: Rip Ford and the Old Southwest*, 22–23.

[19] U.S. War Department, Records Group No. 94.

Mier unresisted."[20] The Rangers did not remain there long, however, for orders arrived from the War Department that they were to reinforce General Winfield Scott, who had led an invasionary force into the Valley of Mexico in the spring of 1847.[21] There the Rangers were to have a special assignment, one that would test their fighting prowess and their pugnacity.

In mid-May the Rangers rode down the Río Grande to a place called Ranchita, where they waited for transportation to Veracruz. While they waited, they probably learned what Scott had done in the Valley of Mexico. The general's advance divisions, moving swiftly through the valley, had driven into Mexico City on September 13 and gained control of the capital by the next morning. Two days later Santa Anna, renouncing the presidency, had fled into the mountains with 5,000 men and another ringing promise to return and drive the Americans back into the sea. The presidency had then devolved on Manuel de la Peña y Peña, who set up an emergency government at Querétaro, some 150 miles northwest of Mexico City. Peña, though a moderate desiring peace, was afraid to sign a treaty because a powerful political faction, opposed to any kind of peace talk, threatened to desert him if he did. Mexican leaders would neither treat nor fight. Many of them promised to prolong the war through endless guerrilla operations.[22]

While Scott and American envoys tried to negotiate with Peña, guerrilla bands stepped up attacks on Scott's long, thin supply line that extended over 260 tortuous miles from Mexico City to Veracruz on the eastern coast. Protecting this supply line from Mexican terrorism was to be the special assignment of the Texas Rangers, who were to proceed to Veracruz at once and "disinfest" the valley of every Mexi-

[20] Ford, *Rip Ford's Texas*, 61.
[21] Hughes, *Rebellious Ranger*, 24.
[22] See Singletary, *The Mexican War*, 71–101.

can bandit and irregular they could find. This was the kind of challenge the Texans loved best (both Scott and President Polk, who had conceived the idea of sending the Rangers against Mexican guerrillas, understood the Texans' temperament better than Taylor did), and they vowed that before they were through, the valley would be littered with dead *guerrilleros*. [23]

In the first week of October four companies of Rangers, along with Adjutant Ford, boarded troop transports at Brazos Santiago and prepared to sail down to Veracruz and locate a regimental campsite. Colonel Hays and the rest of the Ranger force would join them in Mexico on October 17.[24] On board the transports some of the Texans started making trouble before they were out of sight of the Texas coast. One or two of them provoked sailors into fist fights; others—most had never been on a boat in their lives—went exploring like mischievous adolescents. Irate ship captains demanded that Ranger officers control their men. But the officers were causing their own trouble. Even the Rangers' horses were causing trouble. One of them pitched at an Irish sailor, took the man's ear off as "clean as it could have been done by a pair of shears; then chewed it up, and swallowed it." It was so hilarious, said one Ranger, that the Texans could not help but laugh.[25]

After a few days on the rolling, churning sea, the Rangers had little at all to laugh at. For the rest of the voyage the decks were packed with horsemen leaning desperately over the rails or stumbling about trying to comfort one another. "Landsmen do not enjoy being cooped up on a sea-going craft," horseman Ford said, speaking for all. "There was rejoicing when our feet touched on land."[26]

[23] Greer, *Colonel Jack Hays*, 168–70.

[24] New Orleans *Picayune*, October 10, 1847; *Niles National Register* (Baltimore), October 30, 1847.

[25] Ford, *Rip Ford's Texas*, 65–66.   [26] *Ibid.*, 66.

The Rangers did not rejoice long, though. General Robert Patterson, in command at Veracruz, ordered them to set up camp at a virtually uninhabitable place called Vergara, some three miles away on the road to Jalapa, along with another regiment of his "Yankee" division—the 9th Massachusetts Infantry. Apparently the Massachusetts troops had heard about the Texans' propensity to fight their own countrymen if Mexicans were not available: the 9th Infantry sent over half a barrel of whisky along with a peace offering.[27]

Regardless of how much whisky the Rangers consumed, it did not mitigate the nasty conditions at Vergara. A hot, dry wind blew constantly, stirring up loose sand and dust. It was almost impossible to cook or eat there or to keep tents up since the sand would not hold the stakes; the wind kept blowing the tents down anyway. To make matters worse, water was scarce, soon there was no more tobacco or whisky, and a rumor was going around that General Patterson did not think the Rangers could fight the *guerrilleros* in the jungles around Veracruz and that the Texans might have to remain in Vergara until Patterson was ready to march for Mexico City. The Rangers were, of course, bitterly disappointed. It might be a month before the general was prepared to move, and a month in Vergara was worse than a month in hell. With nothing to do except sit around and take pot shots at things, the men became extremely restless. "We were anxious to sustain the reputation of Texas Rangers and not lie around in idleness," the adjutant said, speaking for all.

At length Captain Truitt, Captain Ferguson, and Adjutant Ford called on General Patterson and asked that he send the Rangers against a Mexican guerrilla contingent allegedly operating out of the hacienda of San Juan, about thirty miles away. Although the general doubted that the scout would

[27] New Orleans *Picayune*, October 29, 1847.

accomplish anything, he knew that if the Rangers remained idle much longer they might start their own war in the streets and saloons of Vergara or Veracruz. Reluctantly he permitted them to undertake an expedition.

It was still dark when the Ranger column moved out of camp "at the trot." About mid-morning the horsemen entered a sweltering jungle with parasitic vines that had to be chopped away with bowie knives before they could advance. The Rangers at last reached a waterhole at the edge of a rolling prairie and stopped to rest. Suddenly Adjutant Ford shouted something, then leaped on his horse and galloped away with his pistol blazing. Barely visible on a rise several hundred yards away was a party of guerrillas moving at a killing pace. Mounting on the run, the rest of the Rangers followed the adjutant, shooting recklessly, yelling, spurring their horses faster and faster. On they rode, the guerrillas alternately disappearing and reappearing in the tall grass and ravines, with Ford, not far behind now, trying desperately to draw a bead on the last rider; then came the other Rangers who fired their revolvers and fired again. Suddenly the galloping figure between the two clusters of riders seemed to come apart as the horse stumbled and sent the Ranger flying over its head and into a painful heap on the ground. Captain Truitt, thinking one of the Texans had accidentally killed Ford, started cursing and whipped his wheezing horse toward the fallen rider. But in a moment the adjutant was up cleaning himself off. Signaling to Truitt that he was all right, he leaped on his horse, which apparently was not hurt, and rejoined the chase.

Over the prairie and through the woods the wild riders raced. At last the guerrillas' horses gave out and they had to take shelter at an abandoned ranch. From its buildings they fired at the yipping Texans, who galloped past at full speed while returning the fire, then rode back and dismounted to fight the Mexicans hand to hand.

In a few moments the guerrillas were in complete rout and the skirmishing was over, except for a fist fight two Rangers were having over a dead Mexican's sombrero. When that was settled and all the loot had been fairly divided, the Rangers mounted and set out to find more *guerrilleros*.

A short ride brought them to a fine-looking hacienda where another party of guerrillas was hiding. The Mexicans opened fire, but the Rangers shot several of them dead and chased the rest into the woods where they mysteriously vanished, like Indians. The Texans were disgusted about that, but the rich hacienda made up for the Mexicans they had lost. As they pillaged the place, though, they found some shocking things piled on the marble floor—bloody clothing, forage sacks, and other American articles. Outraged, the Rangers chased the family outside and set the building on fire. Then with their loot they mounted and headed toward Vergara at a fast trot, fearing that a larger enemy force might soon come to overwhelm them. The ride back soon became a race, for "two things are considered uncomfortable by mounted men of pluck," Adjutant Ford mused, "to be in the rear in a charge, or behind in a retreat."[28]

The next day, October 17, Colonel Hays arrived in camp with encouraging news: all the American troops in the Veracruz vicinity were finally going into action. Their orders were to proceed to Jalapa and Puebla, dispersing any guerrilla bands they happened upon, and then to join General Scott in Mexico City. On November 2, 1847, with Adjutant Ford and his newly organized spy company leading the way, the Texas Rangers set out for Jalapa, followed by the 9th

28 Ford, *Rip Ford's Texas*, 66–68, 89.

Massachusetts Infantry, then by regular cavalry and artillery. Like a long, black snake, the United States column crawled through the Mexican sand and dust; thirsty and tired, still following Ford's spy company, it forded rivers that were treacherous with quicksand and shifting mud, hacked its way through humid jungles of vine and bush, and finally reached Jalapa on a warm, sticky afternoon in early November.[29] Regular troops of General Joe Lane's brigade, stationed in the area, aligned themselves along the road to give the Texans "three cheers" as they rode by. "They are a fine body of men and well mounted, with six-shooting rifles," remarked a Pennsylvania volunteer. All the Pennsylvanians believed that the Rangers were "the very men" for Santa Anna's "rascals," who were reported to be holding the town of Izúcar de Matamoros, some one hundred miles southwest of Jalapa and about twenty-five miles south of Puebla.[30]

At Jalapa the Texans found a company of independent "Texas mounted riflemen." These men had a sad and bitter story to tell. It was about the death of their commander, Samuel H. Walker, a "short, slender, spare slouchy man" with fiery red hair and a red beard.[31] Many of Hays's Rangers had known Walker personally, having fought with him in the Monterrey campaign, and they listened tight-lipped as a man told about his death. The captain and his company had come to Mexico back in May, and General Scott had ordered them to stay at Perote to protect American supply convoys from guerrilla attacks. Several months later General Lane's brigade arrived at Perote on its way to garrison duty at Puebla. Lane and Walker planned a joint operation against a Mexican force at Huamantla, said to be under the command of Santa Anna himself. On October 9, Walker and

---

29 *Ibid.*, 75–77; New Orleans *Picayune*, December 9, 1847.
30 J. J. Oswandel, *Notes on the Mexican War, 1846–47–48*, 382; New Orleans *Picayune*, December 9, 1847.
31 Justin H. Smith, *The War With Mexico*, II, 177.

his Texans led some 1,800 regulars down the quiet, shadowy streets of the town. Suddenly Mexicans opened fire from roof tops, and mounted lancers charged in from side streets. The fighting was long and desperate, but the Americans prevailed, driving the Mexicans away to Izúcar de Matamoros. When the smoke had cleared and the men had regrouped, the Texans found Walker lying there in the dust, face down, with bullets in his head and chest. The sight of their captain, dead, caused them to "burst into tears" and swear revenge. During the next month, across the Valley of Mexico, they had fought with bitter hatred and would continue to do so as long as the war lasted. And Hays's Rangers, hearing this, were also moved to tears, and they too swore to avenge Walker's death.[32]

For some of them the chance came the next day. Colonel Hays hand-picked 135 of his best fighters and rode on to Puebla. There General Lane joined him with cannon and a detachment of Louisiana dragoons, and the combined columns, moving by night and resting by day, reached Matamoros on November 24. On the plain outside of town there was a brief engagement between the Texans and a regiment of Mexican Lancers, brilliant in their glittering armor and snapping colors. But the Rangers charged them fiercely, and the Lancers, outfought and outflanked, soon fled.[33]

On November 25 the other Ranger companies under Ford and Chevaille joined Hays near Puebla, and the next day the entire American column, with the Texans in the lead, resumed the march for Mexico City. A regular officer who was most impressed with the Texans wrote in later years that "they certainly were an odd-looking set of fellows, and it

[32] Lane to Adjutant General, October 18, 1847, 30th Cong., 1st sess., *Senate Exec. Doc. 1*, 477–79; Oswandel, *Notes on the Mexican War*, 171–77; Webb, *Texas Rangers*, 115–16.
[33] Lane to Adjutant General, December 1, 1847, 30th Cong., 2d sess., *House Exec. Doc. 1*, 86–89.

seems to be their aim to dress as outlandishly as possible. Bobtailed coats and 'long-tailed blues,' low and high-crowned hats, some slouched and others Panama, with a sprinkling of black leather caps, constituting their uniforms; and a thorough coating of dust over all, and covering their huge beards gave them a savage appearance. . . . Each man carried a rifle, a pair of . . . Colt's revolvers; a hundred of them could discharge a thousand shots in two minutes, and with what precision the Mexican alone could tell."[34]

The Mexican could tell all right; any Mexican in Matamoros—any soldier who had tried to fight these Texans since the war began—could tell with what precision they killed. The Mexican soldier himself believed they were uncanny marksmen who could pick a man off at full gallop over 125 yards away, while he had to shoot one of them at least fives times to kill him. The Mexican would not, of course, admit that he was an extremely poor shot, that his cartridges contained twice as much powder as was necessary, and that this caused his musket to kick bruisingly, which in turn spoiled his aim. Nor would he admit that he feared the recoil of his weapon so much that he often closed his eyes and flinched while firing. No, the explanation lay with the Rangers themselves who were supermen knowing neither fear nor death. But worst of all, the Texans had six-shooters. "The untutored greaser," according to one Ranger, had a "holy awe and superstition . . . in regard for the 'revolver.' They understood the term to mean a turning around and about—a circulator; and were led to believe the ball would revolve in all directions after its victims, run around trees and turn corners, go into houses and climb stairs, and hunt up folks generally."[35] Consequently, Mexican officers had found it next to impossible to keep their men

[34] Albert G. Brackett, *General Lane's Brigade in Central Mexico*, 173–74.
[35] Ephraim M. Daggett, "Adventure with Guerrillas," in Isaac George, *Heroes and Incidents of the Mexican War*, 213.

in line when the Rangers, firing their terrible revolvers and crying the "Texas Yell," came flying down on them.

That yell was another thing. It was awful to hear, even more terrifying in sound than the celebrated "Rebel Yell" of the Civil War. The Texas Yell consisted of a series of wildcat screeches followed by a bloodcurdling yip-yip. "Such yells," said one Texan, "exploded on the air" and "have been heard distinctly three miles off across a prairie, above the din of musketry and artillery."[36]

This hideous yell, the revolver with its ubiquitous bullets, the enormous horses, the tall, bearded supermen from beyond the Río Grande who defied Mexican *escopetas*—no wonder villagers along the road to Mexico City bolted their doors when the Texans rode by. And no wonder citizens in Mexico City were frightened to death when on December 6, Colonel Hays led his Rangers into the heart of the city well ahead of the main column. *"Los Diablos Tejanos! Los Diablos Tejanos!"* cried the Mexicans as they crowded along the streets, like moths drawn to fire, to get a look at the "Texas Devils."[37]

The Rangers had been in town scarcely an hour when they began making trouble. While they waited on the Grand Plaza to get their camp assignments, a Mexican came along with a basket of candy; a Ranger leaned over from his horse and took a handful but refused to pay. The nervous old man shrieked at him, but the Ranger only laughed, so the Mexican hurled a stone at the Texan's head. Almost instantly there was a resounding roar as a revolver appeared in the

[36] Oran M. Roberts, "Texas," in *Confederate Military History* (ed. Clement A. Evans), XI, 146.

[37] Ford, *Rip Ford's Texas*, 81. "Hays's Rangers have come," General Ethan Allen Hitchcock recorded on the day they entered Mexico City, "their appearance never to be forgotten. Not in any sort of uniform, but well mounted and doubly well armed: each man has one or two Colt's revolvers besides ordinary pistols, a sword, and every man his rifle. . . . The Mexicans are terribly afraid of them." Hitchcock, *Fifty Years in Camp and Field* (ed. W. A. Croffut), 310.

Ranger's hand, and the Mexican leaped back as if from a powerful blow, dying before he struck the ground. "There must have been ten thousand people on the Grand Plaza," another Texan recalled. "They were desperately frightened; a stampede occurred. Men ran over each other. Some were knocked into the filthy sewers, all were frantically endeavoring to increase the distance between themselves and *Los Tejanos Sangrientes*—the bloody Texans."[38]

Los Diablos Tejanos. What made them so vicious? They came to Mexico for revenge, they said, but revenge soon became a pretext for acts which transcend human understanding. One evening two Rangers, with bright red bandannas hanging from their hip pockets, started to enter a theater. A Mexican boy ran up, grabbed one of the bandannas, and ran off. The Ranger yelled at him in Spanish, but the boy kept running. So the Texan drew his revolver and killed him. "The ranger," Adjutant Ford wrote later, "recovered his handkerchief and went his way as if nothing had happened."[39]

There was a hatred in Mexico City after that, a growing hatred for those *Diablos Tejanos* who brawled in Mexico's saloons and beat up her men and made violent love to her women. Finally, as the weeks passed and the number of outrages increased, the Mexicans had taken enough. One moonless night a large band of them caught a lone Texan in the streets and stabbed him until "his heart was visible, and its pulsations were plainly perceptible." When the Texans saw his slashed body the next day, they cursed and swore to avenge this ugly deed. That night some twenty-five of them walked deliberately into the "cutthroat" section where the slaying had occurred and murdered from fifty to eighty Mexicans, including young toughs called *léperos.*[40]

[38] Ford, *Rip Ford's Texas*, 81–82.
[39] *Ibid.*, 82.
[40] *Ibid.*, 83–84.

This was too much for the Mexicans. A number of businessmen called at army headquarters and demanded that General Scott keep the Texas Devils off the streets, and the *léperos* themselves swore they would fight any Americans they encountered. If the Rangers were not restrained, the war was going to start up again in the streets of Mexico City, just when the Americans were about to consummate a peace treaty that would permit them all to go home.

When the Rangers shot several more Mexicans in another "affair," General Scott called Colonel Hays to army headquarters. The general was in an ugly mood. "I hold you responsible," he told Hays, "for the acts of your men. I will not be disgraced, nor shall the army of my country be, by such outrages."

"The Texas Rangers are not in the habit of being insulted without resenting it," Hays replied. The Mexicans had thrown rocks at his men, had murdered one of them in cold blood, had attacked others. In his judgment, they had "done right." And he was "willing to be held responsible for it."[41]

But after the general had dismissed him with a stern warning to keep his men in line, Hays was not so sure. What the Texans really needed was to get out of the capital, away from the saloons, the liquor, the hated Mexicans. They needed a campaign, with full-fledged battles in which they could kill Mexicans legitimately. Only that could satisfy them. Only that could keep them out of trouble.

Hays went back to Scott's headquarters and proposed an expedition against one of the toughest bands of *guerrilleros* in Mexico, that of Padre Caledonio de Jarauta, which was hiding out somewhere in the valley east of Mexico City. Over the months this elusive band (along with others led by Juan El Diablo and General Mariano Paredes) had ravaged

[41] Colonel Ebenezer Dumont's Letters, published in the *Indiana Register* and quoted in the *Democratic Telegraph and Texas Register* (Columbia), February 24, 1848.

45

American trains coming from Veracruz, had ambushed cavalry detachments and burned outposts. The Texas Rangers would welcome a chance to prove themselves against the Padre's force, Hays declared, and any other guerrillas they could find. Scott was so anxious to get the Texans out of Mexico City that he approved Hays's plan of operations on the spot.

On the early morning of January 10, 1848, the Rangers left their camp on the southern edge of the city, near San Ángel, and rode into the valley with high hopes of obliterating the infamous *guerrilleros* in a Texas-style fight. First, however, the Rangers had to find them, and that in itself was a formidable task.[42]

The *guerrilleros* were clandestine marauders, but it was no secret that they lived freely among the peons and *léperos* in the villages all across the great valley, gorging themselves and dancing in fiestas that lasted for days. They made the law in that region, and the law was the bullet. They fancied themselves indomitable fighters and dressed in resplendent costumes that kept in awe the pauper youths who idolized them, who lied and stole for them. To the youths they were not men but gods, these *guerrilleros*, in their great sombreros, their velvet jackets so elaborately embroidered by their special señoritas, their skin-tight trousers that were slit open at the sides and fastened by dazzling gold buttons, with tiny silver bells on their boots that jingled as they walked, and huge spurs, and their swords, and the *escopetas* in their hands, and their lassos swung over their shoulders, which they could use with deadly dexterity in close-quarter combat. Yes, they were fighters without equals, they said, and the poor who sheltered them and kept their secrets, the

---

[42] Ford, *Rip Ford's Texas*, 86ff.; Hughes, *Rebellious Ranger*, 40 ff.; Winfield Scott to W. L. Marcy, January 13, 1848, 30th Cong., 1st sess., *House Exec. Doc. 60*, 1067.

youths who worshipped them and the señoritas who loved them, knew in their hearts that no one, not even the Texas Devils coming down the valley, could ever really defeat them.[43]

Yet the Texans, riding in a two-column front behind Hays, with the Lone Star flag and the Stars and Stripes whipping about in the wind overhead, were coming now with every intention of defeating these *guerrilleros* once and for all. Throughout January, 1848, the Rangers searched the whole valley for Padre Jarauta; they skirmished with his detachments at Otumba and San Juan Teotihuacán, but could never capture the Padre himself with his main column, said to be 450 strong. Then in mid-February, riding with a column of United States dragoons under Joe "Old Gritter Face" Lane, the Rangers swooped down on a town called Tulancingo where another guerrilla chief was supposed to be hiding. They found no guerrillas to fight there, but that evening they were given a clue to the whereabouts of the infamous Padre: Zacualtipán, they were told, a village about two days' ride from Tulancingo, was Jarauta's secret headquarters. Moments later the Rangers, followed by Lane's dragoons, mounted in the streets and moved at a gallop into the Mexico night.

The second morning out, they reached the outskirts of Zacualtipán just as the sun was coming up over the mountain peaks. They charged down the early morning streets, taking the *guerrilleros* almost completely by surprise. While the main force under Colonel Hays and General Lane stormed the plaza, a dozen other Rangers leaped from their horses to engage a large body of partially dressed Mexicans who had gathered in an open lot. The Texans fought deftly with revolver and bowie knife in a fast-moving, hand-to-hand

[43] Albert G. Brackett has a description of *guerrilleros*, their nature and their dress, in his reliable study, *History of the United States Cavalry, from the Formation of the Federal Government to the 1st of June, 1863*, 210–13.

fight that lasted about fifteen minutes before the Mexicans broke and fled over the walls and away into the mountains beyond. The Texans then ran up the street to the plaza where a heated battle was raging; yelling like animals, Americans and Mexicans were wrestling and slashing at one another with long knives, were firing into one anothers' faces and stomachs at point-blank range. The killing finally ended at mid-afternoon, with the *guerrilleros* following their Padre down the valley in headlong flight, and Adjutant Ford, who saw the smoking streets littered with corpses, recorded that at least 150 Mexicans "had ceased to feast on *tortillas*" that day.

The Texans were proud of the victory, even if the Padre had gotten away. The next morning they led the dragoons back toward Mexico City, convinced that with this victory their service in Mexico had only begun, that on the day they caught the Padre again or any other guerrilla chief they would fight a battle Mexico would not forget.

As it turned out, Zacualtipán was the last battle for the Texas Rangers in Mexico. On February 2, 1848, a peace treaty had been signed between Mexico and the United States, and when the Rangers reached the capital, the Americans were beginning to evacuate. The Texans' orders were to ride to Veracruz, where transports were waiting to take them home. The order produced a variety of sentiments among the men. "Some felt the full fruition of success had rewarded their labors," a Ranger remembered. Others adopted "the devil-may-care feeling of letting tomorrow take care of itself." But many of the Rangers, believing that they had not achieved a full measure of revenge against Mexico, regarded the armistice as a tragic turn of events and were extremely bitter about having to go home.[44]

---

[44] Ford, *Rip Ford's Texas*, 86–89. See also the reports of Lane and Hays, 30th Cong., 2d sess., *House Exec. Doc. 1*, 89–95, 98–100.

On March 18, 1848, the Texas Rangers rode out of Mexico City and headed for Veracruz. Some ten days later they reached Jalapa, where they heard news that cheered them considerably: General Santa Anna would pass through Jalapa on his way out of the country into exile. The men became quite excited; they would kill Santa Anna; they would . . . . But Colonel Hays warned them that they could do nothing to Santa Anna now, for the war was over and the fallen emperor was, according to the colonel's reports, traveling under a safe-conduct pass from General Scott himself. Hays made them promise to pitch camp nearby and to stay there, then left them under Adjutant Ford and rode over to an estate some miles away where Santa Anna was expected to take supper; the colonel, Ford was told, wanted to have "a few words" with his old enemy.

Hays had been gone barely an hour when the Rangers became quite uncontrollable. The entire regiment was "in a white heat," Ford recalled; "revenge was the ruling passion of the hour" as the Texans started crying for Santa Anna's head.

Adjutant Ford did not know what to do. Colonel Hays was probably the only man who could dissuade the Rangers from their plan to murder Santa Anna when he passed over the road near their camp. It was not that Ford had had a change of heart about Santa Anna. The adjutant would have liked to get a shot at the Mexican himself, but under the circumstances he had to think of the consequences. For should the Rangers gun down Santa Anna when he was leaving the country under a safe-conduct pass, they would all get into serious trouble. Ford explained this to them; he pleaded and reasoned with them and somehow—he would wonder how for years to come—managed to convince them that if they did kill Santa Anna, they would not only dishonor Texas but would all go to prison. Grudgingly they agreed not to harm

49

him if Ford would at least let them get a look at the general as he passed. Ford consented.

Grumbling about their missed opportunities and bad luck, the Rangers aligned themselves on each side of the road and waited. Presently Santa Anna, whose "face blanched a little at the sight of his enemies of long standing," approached in an open carriage, his wife and daughter with him, followed by a Mexican guard of honor brightly dressed in plume and sash. As the carriage passed by, the Texans glared at the Mexican leader with cold hatred, looking as if they wanted more than anything to be turned loose on him or at least to shake their fists at him. Santa Anna seemed to sense their hatred. "He sat erect," a Texan observed; "not a muscle of his face moved; if his hour had come he seemed resolved to meet it as a soldier should." But the Texans did nothing, nothing at all, and after the carriage had disappeared in the trees, they filed back to camp more bitter now than before.[45]

The next day the Rangers joined Colonel Hays at Jalapa and rode on to Veracruz, where on April 29, 1848, all of them except the colonel and Adjutant Ford were mustered out of service in a sad and solemn ceremony.[46] A few days later they boarded troop transports and sailed north for Texas, no doubt spending the humid days at sea reminiscing about the war and their part in it and how much more they could have done had it lasted longer. According to their officers, according to Texans back home, some already gathering at Port Lavaca to give them a rousing welcome reception, and according to contemporary writers already assiduously at work recording their deeds of derring-do, the Rangers had done all that was humanly possible: they had helped whip a

---

[45] Ford, *Rip Ford's Texas*, 101–104.
[46] New Orleans *Delta*, April 24, 1848; U.S. War Department, Records Group No. 94.

nation given to political coercion and persecution, to all those passions of despotism which so violated their Anglo-American heritage of freedom and the natural rights of man. And they had helped give the United States control of the entire American Southwest, including prosperous California. In the short two years the war had lasted, the Texans had "waged hostilities upon a scale they deemed legitimate" and had proven themselves "good citizens and meritorious soldiers."[47]

Yet what about the outrages they perpetrated on the Mexican people?

Said Adjutant Ford: "It was sometimes difficult to restrain these men, whose feelings had been lacerated by domestic bereavements and who were standing face to face with the people whose troops had committed" such "bloody deeds" as massacring Texan prisoners at Goliad and in the ill-starred Santa Fe and Mier expeditions. If the Rangers themselves had indulged in a few excesses, it was because they were an intensely proud band of fighting men who wanted revenge; even if revenge became a cloak for pillage and murder, the Rangers were still honorable men—"good citizens and meritorious soldiers"—who had a "high grade of patriotism for Texas."[48]

So the Texas Rangers have been presented to posterity. No writer has dared to challenge this traditional image, to take them to task for their vainglory and unpredictable violence. Even the venerable Walter Prescott Webb, whose *Texas Rangers* has clearly become a classic study, refused to say much about their worst crimes—their propensity to hang and stab civilian men and ransack their homes, to kill boys under the pretext of revenge for a slain comrade, to fight their own countrymen when Mexicans were not avail-

---

[47] Ford, *Rip Ford's Texas*, 72.
[48] *Ibid.*, 72–73.

able.[49] The same is true of virtually every other study of these men; they may be scolded occasionally for a minor misdemeanor, such as stealing pigs and whisky, but their demonic deeds are either entirely ignored or played down or explained away as the inevitable results of their militant patriotism. Nobody has dared any other explanation. The Texas Rangers could not have been sadists. *Surely* they were not that. *Surely*, as pioneer volunteers representing a democratic nation, they had killed for something beyond a mere love of violence. *Surely*, as frontiersmen imbued with the republican principles of tolerance and Christian love—for they all, according to Ford, knew the historic meanings of their own revolution and professed to believe in the Bible—*surely* then they had been moved to kill civilians by something other than an indigenous racial hatred of Mexicans. *Surely*, unlike the citizen soldiers of revolutionary France, the Texas Rangers had not succumbed to that intoxicating passion of killing just to kill.

It is difficult indeed to consider the possibility that these heroes of the Republic, whose courage and fighting prowess we still revere, regarded war as did the barbarian hordes of Genghis Khan—that war was one occupation in which man could strip himself of all compassion, all diplomacy, and fight with uninhibited fury, as the violent nature of his soul dictated.

[49] For other views of the Texas Rangers in the Mexican War, I urge the reader to examine Webb, *Texas Rangers*, 91–124; Hughes, *Rebellious Ranger*, 22–56; and Greer, *Colonel Jack Hays*, 126–213.

III

Wagon
Trails
West

THE TREATY which ended the Mexican War and ceded New Mexico and California to the United States was consummated just in time for the Anglo-Americans. In February, 1848, the same month in which the treaty was signed (though it would not be ratified until March), John A. Sutter discovered gold in the Sacramento Valley of northern California. When the news got out, rumors flew all over the country from Texas to New England: prospectors were finding millions overnight; there was more gold in California than all the Spanish conquistadors and Texan raiders put together had ever dreamed there could be. Soon the Great Gold Rush was under way, as thousands of adventurers, driven on by that unquenchable American dream of striking it rich in a single, fabulous windfall, set out for California.

A number of Texans also left to make their overnight fortunes in California: Jacob Snively, former Rangers like Ben McCulloch and Walter P. Lane, and scores of other venturers who—like John Joel Glanton—left their destitute wives and children and never came back.[1]

---

[1] Glanton was typical of the restless adventurers who served with Hays in

53

In the meantime, as news of further strikes arrived from California, Texas businessmen became excited too, but for different reasons. The great exodus west, if it could be channeled through Texas, might mean a fortune right here at home. Intoxicated by the thought of that, they pored over old maps trying to find a suitable route across the state, but existing maps were inaccurate and incomplete. In February, 1849, a group of merchants met at Austin and called on Rip Ford, who had done a lot of surveying before the Mexican War and who knew something about Texas geography, to draw up a report on the best overland route to California's gold via Austin and El Paso. Two days later Ford and a friend named S. D. Mullowney submitted a report by Jack Hays who had tried to blaze a trail to El Paso the year before. Unfortunately, Hays's guide had gotten lost, the party had ended up somewhere in Mexico, and when it had finally returned to civilization, Texans had known no more about the region than they had before. Ford told the merchants that few fortune hunters would come through the state until a professional surveyor with a competent guide charted a route through the El Paso country.[2]

At the same time an acquaintance of Ford's, Robert Simpson Neighbors, under orders from the United States Army, was planning to do just that. Hearing that Ford was interested in such a project, Neighbors came to Austin, and when the two men shook hands and sat down for coffee at Ford's home, they were immediate friends.

---

the Mexican War and then left for California's gold fields to make their fortunes. Glanton himself paid his way by killing Apaches and selling the scalps at fifty dollars apiece to Mexican authorities. Some said the scalps were not always Apache. He was killed in an Indian fight at Yuma, Arizona, early in 1850. Walter Prescott Webb and H. Bailey Carroll (eds.), *Handbook of Texas*, I, 693–94.

[2] *Texas Democrat* (Austin), April 15, 1846; Ford, *Rip Ford's Texas*, 113; Frank Brown, "Annals of Travis County and the City of Austin" (MS, Archives, Texas State Library, Austin), chap. 13, p. 42.

Both were active, restless men. Rip Ford, a native of South Carolina, had grown up in Tennessee and migrated to Texas shortly after San Jacinto. He had been a leading spirit in the annexation movement, had practiced medicine (something which impressed Neighbors, since he would need a doctor for his projected expedition), fought Indians, earned himself a great deal of abuse writing pro-Houston editorials in his liberal newspaper, the *Texas Democrat*, and earned a reputation as a fighter with Hays's Rangers in the Mexican War.[3]

Neighbors was equally well known, both for his efforts to consolidate the Democratic party in Texas and for his work as an Indian agent out on the frontier. Some people said that he had more influence over Texas Indians than any other white man of his generation. General William J. Worth, commanding the Department of Texas, believed he did and had chosen him to chart the El Paso country in hopes that he could secure the help of the Comanches, who knew the region better than any white man.

Ford and Neighbors were the same age, thirty-four; both were over six feet tall, with lean, powerful frames and blue eyes. Their personalities were even similar. Ford was loquacious and outgoing (his hands stroking and molding his phrases made him seem a bit more voluble than he actually was); he had an electrifying vitality, too, that drove him relentlessly through tasks regardless of how difficult they were. But what attracted people to him was not his reckless energy; it was his wit, his charming sarcasm which allowed him to make fun of most anything without angering people or hurting their pride.

"The Major," as all of Neighbors' friends knew him, also had humor; in fact, he knew more jokes than any man in the

---

[3] For biographical information on Ford, see my own introduction to *Rip Ford's Texas*, xvii–xlviii.

state, if not the whole Southwest, and could tell them for hours—until his listeners could not bear to laugh any more. His wit was even more sarcastic than Ford's. The Major never smiled while telling his yarns. He never smiled while somebody else was telling a joke either—he never smiled at all—and wherever he went, people were stirred as much by his stubborn pride, his intimidating frowns, his bluntness and determination, as they were by his sarcastic humor.[4]

It was the Major's adventurous spirit, however, that most impressed Ford. The project, as Neighbors described it, promised much excitement. Could the Major use a man who had experience as both a surveyor and a doctor? The Major, with a twinkle in his eye, shook Ford's hand a second time. After making their plans, they agreed to leave on March 2, 1849, from Bernard's Trading Post near present-day Waco.

While Neighbors went out to the Indian reservations to get a few guides, Ford rode on to the trading post where he hired a couple of white men named Doc Sullivan and Alpheus D. Neal. Sullivan was an impetuous and impish little man, always getting into mischief. "He could sing for hours," Ford recalled later, "and not repeat a song." He was "a terror to pretenders and windbags." Neal, his "constant companion," was "a manly specimen" who had never learned the meaning of fear. On the expedition these two would prove to be incomparable, both for the quality of their work and for the devilry they set on foot.[5]

On March 1 Neighbors arrived at the post with a number of Indians who would accompany the expedition. Delaware Jim Shaw would be their interpreter. Joe Ellis and Tom Coshatee, two Shawnees; Patrick Goin, a Choctaw; and John Harry, another Delaware—all of them would serve as hunt-

---

[4] Kenneth Franklin Neighbours, "Robert S. Neighbors in Texas, 1836–1859: A Quarter Century of Frontier Problems" (Ph.D. dissertation, University of Texas, 1955), 9.

[5] Ford, *Rip Ford's Texas*, 115.

ers and do whatever menial tasks were necessary, such as finding suitable campsites and cooking the meals. Buffalo Hump's Comanche band would also go along, with Buffalo Hump acting as guide.

When this motley crowd started west the next day, Ford took an interest in the friendly Comanches, learned many things about their people he had never known before, and recorded these in the journal he kept of the party's operations. For one thing, he learned about the Great Spirit, about signs and charms, and about the medicine Buffalo Hump carried in his buffalo skins.

On the third morning out the chieftain demonstrated his powers in a medicine song. "It was a grand thing, no doubt, to an appreciative audience," Ford wrote. "It stirred up recollections of boyhood—the calling of hogs, the plaintive notes of a solitary bull frog, the bellowing of a small bull, and all that sort of noises. Anon, the awful melody of the sonorous song was reproduced; the next moment the mournful howl of a hungry wolf saluted the ear, which gradually softened into something like the gobble of a turkey. It might have been a choice assortment of Comanche airs gotten up to amuse . . . but it failed to solace his white companions. The performance commenced about an hour before daylight and did little to soothe the slumbers of the morning."[6]

As the party rode that morning, Ford and Neighbors, who had lived with the Comanches for several years, got into a discussion about the Indians' peerless horsemanship. Dismounted, the Comanche was awkward and sluggish, but when he was on a horse he moved with remarkable ease, as if he "took lordship from the animal who was lord of the prairies."[7] War chiefs, Neighbors pointed out, owned great herds of stallions—but no mares, because maleness meant

[6] *Ibid.*, 116.
[7] Paul Horgan, *Great River: The Rio Grande in North American History,* 849.

57

superiority. And each stallion carried his master's essence: when the Comanche broke a wild mustang, he roped and threw it and, covering its nostrils with his mouth, exhaled his breath and his controlling spirit into the animal.

They got these horses by raiding ranches in Mexico when the moon was full in September—the time of the Mexico moon, when the summer rains were over and cool winds began to blow across the prairies of wild, succulent grasses. After a ceremony of songs and dances and tales of war, Comanche warriors set out along the Comanche war trail— which seemed like "a great chalk line on the map of west Texas from the Llano Estacado to the Río Grande"—heading for Mexico to take horses.[8]

Ford, as Neighbors said he would, also learned about Comanche cruelty. On the fourth day out the party stopped at Shanaco's camp on Spring Creek above the mouth of the Colorado, and Rip saw something there he would never forget—a white woman whom the Indians had taken prisoner as a child and had raised as one of their own. She had auburn hair, blue eyes, and almost translucent cheeks that were marred by deep slashes—slashes she had apparently inflicted on herself as an indication of grief when her Indian husband had died. She seemed extremely morose, and Ford was overwhelmed by pity for her—a woman "now rendered forever desolate and disconsolate by being made a captive by savage Indians, and forced to become the wife of a barbarian—not only his wife but his menial, his slave, to be the humble servitor of his shams and caprices, to be punished for a seeming disposition to disobey his behests, to be beaten, lassoed, and pulled through prickly pear, with a rope among the middle, and filled full of thorns to gratify the vengeance of one possessing less pity than a brute." When Ford fought the Comanches several years later, he said the

8 *Ibid.*, 851.

58

"woman with auburn hair, slashed cheeks, and a countenance of extreme sorrow appeared to lead him. She was before his mind's eye, and he struck for her and for vengeance."[9]

It may have been at the encampment on Spring Creek that Sullivan, making eyes at the Indian women, almost got himself killed. He called them around him and proceeded to give them a revealing lecture about the advantages of marrying a white man. When the warriors found out about this, they "swore at Sullivan considerably," threatening to kill him if he ever bothered their women again. They soon came to the conclusion, however, that he was crazy and so not responsible for what he did. Sullivan quickly took advantage of their "silly supposition" and went around sticking pins in the Indians, making them "cut capers very unusual for braves to perform."[10]

Major Neighbors and Ford warned him that he was going to get into trouble again, but Sullivan would not listen. One morning, Ford recalled, Sullivan "notified the Indian public that he would give a performance, free of charge, and invited a general attendance. He had a good audience. He played the buzzard, performing feats imitative of those customary to that melancholy bird in near proximity to a dead horse. He next illustrated the antics of a lizard. He went off on all fours at a brisk gait, ensconced himself behind a log. He would peep over the log, and drop out of sight in the twinkling of an eye. The sight of his contorted face, and his white eyes as they danced in his head, produced shouts of laughter. Anything more ludicrous has seldom been witnessed. He sang a lisping song—'Miss Julia was very peculiar' was the chorus. The Comanches did not understand a word, yet they applauded, and laughed immoderately. One

9 Ford, *Rip Ford's Texas*, 119–20.
10 *Ibid.*, 117.

young warrior laughed himself almost into convulsions. His friends carried him off, fearing he would make himself sick."[11]

Later, when the party was on the move again, an Indian named Tall Tree, who had replaced Buffalo Hump as guide, called Sullivan's bluff. Sullivan was *not* "loco," Tall Tree announced, and ordered him to fetch the Indian some water from a nearby spring. "A large row commenced then and there," Ford said. "Sullivan gesticulated and swore in English, Spanish, and a sprinkling of Caddo. Tall Tree called down anathemas upon Sullivan in pure Comanche, bad Spanish, English, and in tongues unknown to all of us." They might have killed each other had Major Neighbors not interfered, sending Tall Tree away to feast on horse meat by himself and warning Sullivan to leave the Indians alone, lest he end up with his throat slit. Grumbling, Sullivan agreed to behave—for a while anyway.[12]

By now the party had crossed Brady's Creek, where Neal had gotten lost while out hunting for food. The others gave him up for dead (hardly able to know that he had been picked up by a band of friendly Comanches and was now on his way back to the settlements). From Brady's Creek the party followed the Concho up to its head, then rode past the Flat Rock water holes on their way toward the Horsehead Crossing of the Pecos. Just beyond the water holes a wet norther unexpectedly struck, blowing sleet and snow against them with raging force. They stumbled blindly on, finally reaching a hackberry thicket where they made camp. All that night they sat huddled around a small, smoking fire, worn out and miserably cold and further depressed because in a day or two their supplies would be exhausted.

The next day they pushed on through the Castle Mountains, then dropped down the graveled, sandy slope and swam their horses at the Horsehead Crossing. Now their supplies were gone, and as they headed almost due south toward the Río Grande, they had to live on wild turkey, deer, prairie dog, or, when these were not available, on horse meat. Although the Indians considered horse meat a delicacy and ate it with great relish, the white men could not stomach it. In Ford's opinion, "It tasted like a sweaty saddle blanket smells at the end of a day's ride."[13]

Down now to what Ford called "starving man's luck," the riders drove themselves over the Pah-cut Range (Davis Mountains), threaded their way through Carrizo Pass which wound southward "like a crooked knife wound," then bore off to the southwest, their strength waning from polluted water and lack of food.[14] When they finally reached the Río Grande, they were in a state of near delirium.

"I'm glad we are on the Río Grande," said Sullivan, who was less affected than the others.

"The Río Grande, where is it?" Ford asked with a thick tongue.

"You confounded fool, you have been riding on its banks for more than two miles."

"Is that so? I thought it was a pond."[15]

That evening Delaware Jim Shaw killed and roasted a deer whose rich wild meat restored their strength a little. One of the Comanches contributed a snake. Still near starvation, they set out at "a good pace" the next morning and a few days later reached the village of San Elizario, then pushed over the remaining few miles to El Paso. There they ate as they had never eaten before. In twelve hours Ford and Sullivan, in addition to three regular meals, "counted up forty-two eggs they had eaten, besides other things."[16]

While Sullivan and the Indians rested in an open lot be-

13 *Ibid.*, 124.
14 Hughes, *Rebellious Ranger*, 67.
15 Ford, *Rip Ford's Texas*, 125.   16 *Ibid.*, 127.

tween a saloon and a dry goods store, Ford and Neighbors went to meet a living American legend, the Great Western, a huge powerful woman who operated a hotel and gambling house. She could whip any man, fair fight or foul, could shoot a pistol better than anybody in the region, and at poker could out-play (or out-cheat) the slickest professional gambler. There are many stories regarding her background, but one has it that she had fallen in love with Zachary Taylor back in Florida and had followed him to Texas. When war began and "Old Rough and Ready" led his army into Mexico, she came to El Paso and bought a hotel. One day a man fresh from the battle of Buena Vista came running into her hotel crying that Taylor had been badly defeated. The Great Western floored the courier with a powerful blow between the eyes as she bellowed, "You damned son of a bitch, there ain't Mexicans enough in Mexico to whip old Taylor!"[17] According to gossip, she was still in love with the general and would let no man touch her. Not that anybody really wanted to, for as a saying went, it would require some mutation of man and gorilla to handle her anyway.

As anyone would, the two explorers approached this woman "in a polite, if not humble, manner," explained what they were doing in El Paso, asked about the conditions there and in the surrounding territory, then rejoined their party.[18]

They spent the next week or so studying and revising the maps they had drawn on the ride from Bernard's Trading Post. Neighbors' column left El Paso in May, moved swiftly past Alamo Springs and through the Guadalupe Mountains, then followed the meandering Pecos River down to Horsehead Crossing.[19] Near the crossing they met a wagon train

[17] George Washington Trahern, "Texas Cowboy from Mier to Buena Vista" (ed. A. Russell Buchanan), *Southwestern Historical Quarterly*, LVIII (July, 1954), 85.

[18] Ford, *Rip Ford's Texas*, 126.

[19] *Texas Democrat* (Austin), June 23, 1849; Kenneth F. Neighbours,

heading for California and had dinner with the emigrants. While they sipped coffee afterwards, Tall Tree started making a shield. While doing so, he indulged "in some very peculiar orgies," emitting noises like "a Mexican hog . . . in a very violent passion. There was a 'chomping' and a 'gritting' of teeth, and a great deal of grunting, and other hoggish capers" that frightened many of the emigrants out of their wits and caused some "horrid oaths to be sworn."[20]

The next day the party rode through the Castle Mountains, passing another wagon train heading west near the headwaters of the Concho, then set out for Fort San Saba. Near there the explorers encountered "quite an old gentleman" leading a pack animal. When he saw the Indian guide, he leaped back. "Oh!" he cried, "gentlemen, you certainly wouldn't hurt a poor lone man—there are seventy men behind: go take them." This, Ford said, "was addressed to five hungry chaps, who had hardly strength to have committed *petit larceny* on a hen-roost!"[21] After the "antique wayfarer" had hurried off, still not convinced that they were friends, the riders met another wagon train, got some rations from it in return for Sullivan's services as guide to El Paso, then set out for San Antonio, where Neighbors was supposed to make his report to the army.

The party reached San Antonio on the morning of June 2, having covered the 1,160 miles out to El Paso and back in approximately three months. As they rode through the main plaza, Ford became aware that people were staring at him. When he dismounted and tied up in front of a dining room, he looked at himself and knew what the trouble was. He had on "a pair of old drawers and a breechclout, no coat, and a

"The Expedition of Major Robert S. Neighbors to El Paso in 1849," *Southwestern Historical Quarterly*, LVIII (July, 1954), 54.

[20] Ford, *Rip Ford's Texas*, 127.

[21] *Texas Democrat* (Austin), June 16, 1849.

shirt chock full of the free-soil element." A few moments
later the proprietor of the dining room threatened to throw
this "vagabond" out, but "the boys played a confidence game
on him by reciting the number of murders 'Old Rip' had
committed. To purchase silence the unfortunate victim set
out the drinks."[22]

In the meantime Neighbors submitted his report (which
Ford had helped him prepare) to General George M. Brooke,
commanding the Eighth Military Department of Texas. The
general compared the report to one made by Lieutenant W.
H. C. Whiting, who had blazed a more southerly trail to El
Paso (later called the lower route), while Ford and Neighbors charted what was called the upper route.[23] The general
thought the Neighbors trail was the more practicable of the
two and complimented the Major for a job well done. Neighbors in turn praised Rip Ford, whom "I found an energetic
and able assistant, the services rendered by him were important to the successful termination of the expedition. I
cheerfully recommend him to your favorable notice."[24]

In mid-June, Ford returned to Austin and published an
account of the expedition in the *Texas Democrat*, giving the
exact route taken and describing in detail the fertility of the
soil and the abundance of natural resources in the west Texas
region.[25] He even told the group of merchants he represented
that, if they wanted a real windfall, they should build a railroad through the El Paso country. This would bring more
gold hunters through Texas than would a mere wagon road,
and would help settle west Texas, whose resources, if uti-

[22] Ford, *Rip Ford's Texas*, 128.
[23] A. B. Bender, "Opening Routes Across West Texas," *Southwestern
Historical Quarterly*, XXXVII (October, 1933), 116–35.
[24] Robert S. Neighbors, "The Report of the Expedition of Major Robert
S. Neighbors to El Paso in 1849" (ed. Kenneth F. Neighbours), *Southwestern
Historical Quarterly*, LX, (April 1957), 532.
[25] "Report of Dr. John S. Ford—upon the practicability of a Route from
Austin to El Paso del Norte," *Texas Democrat* (Austin), June 23, 1849.

lized, would make Texas one of the more prosperous states in the Union.[26]

The businessmen thanked Ford for his able suggestion. A railroad through west Texas was something to think about all right. For the moment, though, they were more interested in the work of Ford and Neighbors in opening the El Paso Trail. It was indeed a considerable achievement, for in August alone over 4,000 people passed through El Paso on their way to California. In addition, the trail extended Texas' jurisdiction out to the Staked Plains and brought eastern New Mexico within easy reach of the Texas government. Now the old dreams were back again: westward expansion, the lucrative Santa Fe trade, a Greater Texas. The Texas legislature at its next session decided to act on an earlier proposal to divide the El Paso country into counties and sent Major Neighbors to organize them. Neighbors finished his work by the first of March, 1850, then rode up to organize the country around Santa Fe too, while the Texas government—and the entire Texas business community—must already have been correcting their maps to bring the Santa Fe trade through El Paso and east across the land which Ford and Neighbors had charted.

But most New Mexico citizens no more wanted to join Texas than they did Mexico; they wanted to establish an independent state, a free state, and when Neighbors arrived with his surveying instruments and his Texas drawl, they protested angrily. Then United States authorities intervened—it was the abortive Snively Expedition all over again—and Neighbors' efforts were blocked. There followed mutual recriminations and threats of war between Texas and the United States government—Texas at one point even threatened to secede from the Union—until at last the whole controversy was resolved as part of the Compromise of

26 Ford, *Rip Ford's Texas*, 129.

1850. According to the compromise, Texas surrendered all claim to eastern New Mexico, and the federal government, in return, assumed the ten-million-dollar debt Texas had incurred during the Republic. "It is no strain upon truth to assume that the expedition of Major Neighbors was a factor in these important events," Ford wrote in his memoirs.[27] Neither Ford nor anybody else in Texas was exactly ecstatic about the settlement. But ten million dollars in assumed debts was nothing to sulk about either. It was more than any of the Texans' other westward thrusts had yielded them.

[27] *Ibid.*

IV

Rangers
on the
Border

ORD had been back from El Paso scarcely two months
when a United States Army courier on a humid August afternoon came to his residence in Austin with a
note that Colonel John Pitts wanted him at headquarters.
Ford, who kept up with current events, had an idea what was
bothering the colonel. For three years renegade Comanches
and Mexican outlaws had terrorized the area between the
Nueces River and the Río Grande. Swift and cunning, these
bands had outwitted the small regular army with its book
tactics, had ambushed and scattered citizen posses, and had
forced the frightened settlers to co-operate with them. Now
the army was going to fight fire with fire: at army headquarters Colonel Pitts told Ford that General George M. Brooke
wanted him to get up a company of men who had fought with
Jack Hays in the Mexican War—veteran fighters who could
scalp and torture like the Indians, who could ride and shoot
like the Mexicans—and take them into the region to restore
order.[1]

Aching to get in the saddle, Ford accepted the colonel's

[1] Unless otherwise cited, the account of Rip Ford's rangers on the border
is based on Ford, *Rip Ford's Texas*, 141–89.

proposal at once and hurried out to start signing up recruits. In less than two weeks he had raised nearly a hundred men, who were sworn into United States service in Austin on August 23, 1849. Armed with long-barreled Colts and bowie knives, dressed in motley and often outlandish "uniforms," these Rangers were as formidable-looking as any Jack Hays had ever led.

Early in September the company trotted out of Austin and, after five days of hard and continuous riding, reached H. L. Kinney's ranch, some eight miles below Corpus Christi. While the men built fires to keep warm in the cold front that had moved in that morning, Captain Ford had a talk with Kinney, who reported having seen a fresh Indian trail a few miles up the Nueces River Valley. Ford decided to follow the trail the next morning.

It had begun to rain quite hard now. Through the night the Rangers huddled in their soaked bedding trying to stay warm. Soon a cold wind began to blow through the woods, freezing to icicles the water that dripped from the trees. The cold was almost unbearable. The only way one could stay warm was to move about, so the captain gave the order to mount up long before daybreak. Tired, hungry, and numb from the cold, the Rangers formed in column and headed up the valley. Now there were no thoughts of Indians, only of making it to Laredo and warmth and hot food.

It took six days to get there—six days of fording creeks swollen from the heavy rains, wading, swimming, and splashing through mud and bogs, while the winds blew and blew harder still. When they dismounted at last in Laredo, they were all suffering from exposure and a few from frostbite.

While they recovered, Captain Ford, who did not have time to be sick, rode up and down the Río Grande talking with settlers about Indian depredations, then returned to camp to write a long report stating that so extensive were the Indian raids that "a general dread prevailed everywhere" in the lower Río Grande region. It was "impossible to procure Mexican laborers to work in the fields on the east bank of the Río Grande." Moreover, a "large number of Texas citizens, of Mexican origin, and paying State taxes upon their lands, were living on the west bank of the Río Grande in consequence of the inadequate protection given them."

The captain had found that not all the raids were made by Comanches. One night not long ago Ramon Falcon's band of Mexican outlaws rode into Brownsville by the full of the moon, murdering a number of civil and military officials. One of them was Colonel Trueman Cross of the United States Army who had been a good friend of Ford's. "Should the villain who bathed his hands in the blood of one of the best officers in the army, fall into my hands," Ford said angrily, "I shall hang him to the first convenient tree, as an act of retributive justice for his crimes."[2]

The captain meant what he said. In a few days he was out tacking up notices that his Texas Rangers intended to restore peace and order to a region where the law so far had been how well you could shoot or could ride.

Late in October the captain rode down to Mier, Mexico, to gather information on a Seminole band that was supposed to be involved in the Texas raids. The first night he was there Mexican customs officials uncovered an American smuggling ring, accused the Texas Ranger of being one of the ringleaders, and notified Washington about it. The Secretary of War then ordered General George M. Brooke, commanding the Department of Texas, to arrest Ford, but the general insisted that he was innocent and finally got the charge removed. Rip was irate. He could prove his innocence, he said. On the night the ring was arrested, he had slept in the house

2 *State Gazette* (Austin), December 12, 1857.

of Margarita García, better known as "the Pearl of Mier," who would vouch for his character. "There were several other ladies there," Ford said. "They played on the guitar and sang, and all retired at a late hour."

A week later the captain returned to the Ranger camp outside Laredo and immediately issued an order that created quite a stir among the undisciplined Texans. They were going to drill. That was right, drill: learning to ride in parade formation and, what was worse, to march. Who ever heard of horsemen marching on foot, the men cried, insisting that shooting at targets instead of Comanches was an unforgivable waste of time and ammunition. Most shut up, however, when drillmaster Ford announced that any man who refused to train would be punished in the worst way: on a scout he would be left behind as a camp guard, which to fighting men was awful, was embarrassing, was the lowest form of duty. The next day two malcontents dropped out of drill, announcing that they were through with it; they had enlisted to shoot Indians, not to march about keeping lines straight. But when the angry captain reduced them to camp guards and told them they could not fight for a month, they almost cried, begging him to restore them to the ranks—they would drill, they would do anything—but Ford, a stern disciplinarian, was recalcitrant. It was a good lesson. After that, the drills were executed in silence.

One day a patrol found Indian signs and galloped back to camp shouting that Comanches were out there. A scout quickly organized and flew off into the brush. The excited riders, led by the captain himself, soon came to an open prairie where they stopped to rest their lathered horses. A Ranger told everyone to be quiet for a moment; he thought he had heard a roar like thunder off in the west, but it could not be, for the sky was clear. Then several others heard it too, a continuous roar, louder than thunder now and coming nearer. Presently, two riders—the patrol's rear guard—came galloping across the prairie closely pursued by a herd of stampeding wild mustangs. Frantically, the Rangers formed a hollow square around their pack mules, waited until the horses were in range, then fired for their lives, picking off the leading horses one by one until the animals broke their stride, then turned back on one another in wild disorder.

Shouting and firing overhead, the Rangers started after them on foot and drove them off, only to look back and see their own mules and horses running off in the opposite direction. Cursing, the Texans chased after them. That night one could still hear them tramping about in the distant thickets calling for their horses and slapping stubborn mules back to the bivouac.

When all the animals had been rounded up, Captain Ford decided that further pursuit was useless and led his grumbling troops back toward camp. On the way Private Henderson Miller, who was suffering from a sunburned face and blistered lips, hoisted a makeshift umbrella, much to the disgust of the other Rangers, who abhorred any show of effeminacy or dandyism. They didn't do anything about it just then, perhaps because the captain was present.

The next day Captain Ford and two other men went hunting in the woods just above the ranger camp. Suddenly they heard the pop of revolvers and cheers back to their left.

"The Indians have attacked the camp!" one yelled, turning his horse and drawing his six-shooter.

Ford held up his hand and listened to the shouts. "No such thing," he said, grinning, "the boys are shooting Henderson Miller's umbrella." The captain was right, for when they got back to camp, they found Ranger Miller looking painfully (and rather sheepishly) at a pile of torn cloth that had been an umbrella, while the other Rangers were lounging innocently around their tents. "The captain, for once, let the matter pass unnoticed," Ford recorded in his memoirs. "He did not see how he could remedy the affair, and thought that silence was wisdom."

Weeks passed and still the daily patrols found no sign of the renegade Indians. The men became bored and restless. Ford knew better than to keep them cooped up in camp with nothing to do but drill and started giving them passes to Laredo. The Rangers deeply appreciated the opportunity to get drunk, and they told their captain so, told him they thought he was a great officer, even though he didn't drink, because he knew what a man needed now and then, and that was a good binge. To show their appreciation, they tried and did the impossible: "While in town they made no braggadocio demonstration," Ford said, looking on with unreserved pride. "They did not gallop through the streets, shoot and yell," as had been the custom of all Texas Rangers since the days of the Republic. This, of course, was a pleasant surprise to local merchants who feared for their lives and property—and their women—when the Rangers came to town looking for excitement. When relieved businessmen thanked the captain over and over, he told them that his men had "a specie of moral discipline which developed moral courage. They did right because it was right." They did right because the captain had threatened personally to thrash any man who stepped out of line.

On the way back from Laredo one day, a party of Rangers, including the captain himself, spotted a couple of riders moving suspiciously across the faraway horizon. Thinking they were Indians, the Rangers whooped and gave chase, careening through the mesquite and prickly pear, coming soon to a lagoon which the mysterious riders had crossed after leaving their saddles and saddlebags on the bank. The

Texans looked at the bags, then looked at each other. They were mailbags.

"Come—get your mailbags," the captain bawled out. "We're not Indians!"

But the frightened riders kept on going, and when they reached Goliad days later, the local newspaper carried their story, describing in graphic detail how they had eluded a band of bloodthirsty savages without falling for their cunning tricks. "They couldn't fool me with their English!" one boasted.

The Rangers were rather disgruntled over the whole affair. They had joined up to fight Indians, yet for months now they had done nothing except cavort around the countryside fighting mustangs and mail carriers. The new year 1850 came and the story was still the same: no Indians. In February the Rangers re-enlisted for six months only after Captain Ford promised them a fight and soon.

In March the command selected a new permanent camp seventy miles southeast of Laredo on the road to Ringgold Barracks and named the camp San Antonio Viejo—Old San Antonio. The men spent nearly two months pitching tents in a grove of oak trees, building cabins in which to store supplies, and erecting a low wooden wall around the camp.

It was May now and the days were warm and humid— perfect weather for hunting Indians. Captain Ford organized a scout of forty picked men, including First Lieutenant Andrew Walker, Sergeant David Level, Private Mat Nolan, a "sprightly lad" who was the company bugler, and the captain's aide-de-camp, a nervous little Mexican named Don Francisco de la Garza Falcon, whom the Rangers condescendingly called "the Monkey." In a staff meeting that night, Ford said he would scout the country above Laredo, then would turn east and head for Corpus Christi, where he hoped to draw six-shooters for the company since the ones in stock were unserviceable. After that he would head back to San Antonio Viejo.

At daybreak on May 5, 1850, the Rangers trotted out of camp to seek out the Comanches. About fifteen miles out the captain split the force into two columns, one under himself and the other under Lieutenant Walker. While Walker's column moved in a northerly direction, Ford's party rode to the Nueces River, followed it for a few miles, then rode down a tributary, San Roque Creek, and encamped in a clearing near the water. Sergeant Level and another Ranger named Jack Sharpe were stationed in the trees with strict orders to keep quiet and look out for Indians moving about under cover of darkness. About 2:00 A.M. the pickets heard coyotes barking nearby and decided to investigate—after all, those might be Comanches barking. Crawling along on their stomachs, the two Rangers found that a gang of coyotes had treed a leopard. They forgot their orders and came charging out of the brush screaming and firing their revolvers at the coyotes, which fled for their lives, then killed and dressed the leopard. In a few minutes the Ranger camp was alive with men shouting and running about looking for the pickets. When Level and Sharpe came back to camp with a dead leopard, Captain Ford was beside himself with anger, bawled them out for such indiscreet proceedings, and sent them to their bedrolls. Then he told the men to get some rest —they had a hard day ahead of them—but they were all too excited to get any sleep that night.

The next morning, just as they were preparing to ride, Lieutenant Walker's column arrived. The troopers were dead tired and their horses were nearly jaded. Walker told Ford that they had stumbled on a band of Comanches by accident and had chased them for two days through dry creek beds, across prairies, and through the mesquite and prickly pear, but could not catch them. Walker was extremely irritated about it, but the captain assured him that they would find plenty of Indians on the scout. He was sure of it.

After Walker's men had eaten breakfast and had fed and watered their horses, the united force rode down the Nueces, following it for about four days before reaching the Comanche Crossing about daybreak on May 12, 1850. Here they found a fresh Indian trail. Sensing a battle, the men were hardly able to control themselves. Following the trail quietly and nervously, they came soon to the Nueces Valley where they found a fresh campsite in a small clearing near the river. The Indians were perhaps an hour's ride ahead, and the Rangers moved off at the trot. After fording a creek, the captain with Walker and Level rode on ahead and came to a slight elevation where they sighted the Comanches moving leisurely through a field of prickly pear not four hundred yards away.

"Here they are!" the captain yelled. And his Rangers came up on the run.

The Indians were game: they formed in line of battle and fitted their arrows.

The Rangers, armed with Mississippi rifles (muzzle loaders), formed a line, too, and listened to their captain give them instructions. "Ride up to the right and rear of an Indian, and he cannot use his arrows. . . ."

A Ranger interrupted him, pointing at the Comanche chief who was riding along in front of the Rangers about thirty yards away.

"Be steady boys!" Ford cried. "He wants to draw your fire and then charge you with the lance!"

But the Rangers couldn't wait. Sergeant Level fired his revolver and blood spurted from the chief's arm. He wheeled his horse about and threw his lance, then led his shrieking warriors toward the Texans. Raising their rifles, the Rangers waited for the order.

"Charge!" Ford bellowed.

A terrible screech burst on the air, followed by high-pitched yip-yips as the Texas Rangers leaped forward to engage the warriors hand to hand. Over the din of musketry and war whoops could be heard the strained yells of leaders exhorting their men to die, as a confusing mass of fighters rolled and twisted around in the prickly pear, the Indians jabbing with spears while the Texans stabbed with bowie knives and clubbed with rifle butts. Soon the Indians withdrew to an elevation a few hundred yards away and started lofting their arrows—shooting them at an angle so they would rain down on the Rangers' heads. Returning the fire, the Texans scrambled for cover, but not before a man fell dead with an arrow in his head and Captain Ford's horse dropped with one through its neck.

Out of arrow range now, the Texans lay down on the ground and started picking off the Comanches with accurate rifle fire. The Indians, running this way and that in wild disorder, began to wail mournfully; the Rangers thought this was a sullen shout of defiance until Ford said they were crying over dead warriors. Then they took off at full speed, and the yipping Texans came after them. Over the prairie and through a creek bed they went, the Texans firing recklessly at the bobbing figures in front of them who moved in a zigzag pattern in a desperate effort to get away. The chase finally ended when the red men galloped into a heavily timbered region and seemed to vanish. For hours the Texans swarmed about in the woods searching for a sign, but in vain. They were not at all happy about it; the victory was incomplete since some of the Comanches had gotten away.

As the Rangers trotted back over the battlefield, the captain's aide, the Monkey, jumped from a tree wanting to know what had happened. Ford and Mat Nolan looked at him and could hardly keep from laughing. When the fight had opened, the Monkey had raced past Nolan, who told him he was heading in the wrong direction, but the don didn't think so and kept right on running even though Nolan threatened to shoot him for desertion. Far to the rear the Monkey climbed a tree and stayed there. He was mighty glad it was over now, he said, climbing on his pony and joining Ford and Nolan, and he was glad, too, that he was on the winning side.

On the ride back to San Antonio Viejo, Ford overheard the Monkey giving a graphic account of the fight to one of the men.

"Notwithstanding the *capitán* was on a fine horse and I on a pony, we were side by side—*parejitos*—all the time. I fired all my cartridges and went into them with my knife."

"What?" said the Ranger. "With nothing but your knife?"

"*Con nada solo mi puro belduque*—with nothing but my naked knife."

That evening the rear guard sighted a large body of Comanches, seventy or eighty strong, tracking the Ranger column (the same Indians the Texans had defeated the previous day returning now with reinforcements). Captain Ford ordered his men to form in line of battle, but the Comanches refused to fight. For the next several days the red men followed the Rangers, waiting for a chance to surprise them. But Ford kept his men battle ready night and day, and the Indians finally rode off.

On May 26 the column encamped near Fort Merrill, which was located a few miles west of Corpus Christi and commanded by Captain J. B. Plummer of the regular army. That night "the moon was full and sent a flood of silver light upon a beautiful landscape," the captain recalled. The full moon, however, was an ominous sign. Just after midnight the Comanches returned and attacked the pickets, and all the firing and thrashing about brought the Rangers out of their bedrolls on the run.

Captain Ford, fearing an ambush, leaped on his horse bareback and darted into the brush, firing at shadows and cracking twigs, but the Indians had gone when he reached the picket line. Returning to camp, Ford saw a couple of Rangers helping Mat Nolan, whose legs and feet were bleeding profusely, back to his bedroll. The youthful bugler said he had gotten so carried away during all the excitement that he ran barefoot through a field of prickly pear to get a shot at the retreating Indians.

The next morning before breakfast Captain Ford and young Ed Burleson rode over to Fort Merrill to tell Captain Plummer what had happened.

"What!" the captain exclaimed. "Indians so near my post? I thought it was you Texans fighting among yourselves."

When Ford and Burleson returned to camp, they found the Rangers crowded around a regular soldier who had accompanied the scout. It appeared that the soldier, whom the Rangers had nicknamed "Luny," had cut off the head of a dead Indian and taken it to his bedroll. The Texans did not know what to make of it: scalping was all right—they had done it themselves—but cutting off the whole head was a little too much. A few of them were convinced that the soldier was downright crazy and were going to run him out of camp until a Ranger who liked Luny persuaded them differently.

"Now boys," the Ranger said, "that Indian sneaked into camp expecting to steal our horses and to whip us, no doubt. He got himself killed . . . [and] the regular soldier served him like David did Goliath: he chopped his head off with a butcher knife." The Ranger later confided to Captain Ford that "that Indian was the 'worse broken up' man in the world."

That afternoon the Texans broke camp and moved out at the trot. They had gone about ten miles when the front scout, Bill Gillespie, reported seeing the Comanches drawn up for battle in a grove of mesquite trees just ahead. With Captain Ford leading the way, the Rangers charged the Indians, who then mounted and fled. The Rangers gave chase, overtook the red men in a grassy arroyo, and went to work with their bowie knives. It was a short fight and a Ranger victory, with four Indians killed, seven wounded, and the rest chased into the nearby woods. The Texans sustained losses too: Private Gillespie died with an arrow in his side, two others were wounded, and Sergeant Level was missing. For over an hour the men roamed the brush looking for him, then the captain found him bent over a dead horse.

"Level, what is the matter?"

"Damn them," he said with clenched teeth, "they've shot my horse."

"Oh, is that all?"

"No, they've shot me too."

The captain dressed Level's wound himself, put him behind Lieutenant Walker on Walker's horse, and strapped Level to the saddle.

The column returned to San Antonio Viejo without further incident. In a couple of days Ford received a note from General Brooke congratulating the Rangers for a successful campaign.[3]

During the rest of the summer Ford's company patrolled the Nueces River Valley but found only one or two Comanche hunting parties, which they chased happily over the prairies. While the captain was out on one such patrol, a

[3] *Ibid.*

daring Comanche band attacked San Antonio Viejo, but a small garrison under Samuel Highsmith, firing their Colts with remarkable accuracy, managed to drive them off. After that, Ford thought it advisable to change camps, and early in September the company set out for Laredo during a stiff norther. It had been raining steadily for days, and the Río Frío was rampaging. Could it be crossed? A rider moved to midstream but the powerful current swept him off his horse and nearly drowned him. Another rider, with one end of a rope tied to his saddle and the other end wrapped around a tree, waded in, slipped, swam, fought his way to the other bank, and finally tied the rope to another tree.

Then one by one, pulling their horses with them, the Rangers inched their way along the rope, thrashing and kicking in the freezing water. Miraculously, they all made it across. But when they got to Laredo, half the company, including Captain Ford, was hospitalized with pneumonia. Lieutenant Walker and Lieutenant Burleson took command and selected Los Ojuelos as the new campsite.

While Ford was in the hospital, Lieutenant Walker led a successful scout against the Comanches, defeating them in a running battle near Cat Creek. Several weeks later, in January, 1851, Lieutenant Burleson, leading another patrol, fought the Comanches on the Nueces River near the San Antonio–Laredo road. According to Captain Ford, who visited the battleground a month or so later, "this was one of the most closely contested Indian fights that ever occurred in Texas." The ground "was literally covered with arrows."

Ford's company made a few more scouts after that but found no Indians (although they did chase a band of Mexican outlaws over half of Webb County and on across the Río Grande). Apparently the Comanches, convinced that they could do little as long as the Rangers guarded the Río Grande country, had returned to their hunting grounds up on the Staked Plains. For the first time in over three years, the settlers could farm their lands in peace. "Commerce was brisker than heretofore," the captain noted, "the roads less dangerous to travel; in fact, a good time seemed to be dawning upon the denizens of southern and southwestern Texas."

As far as Ford was concerned, the Texas Rangers had done all they could do and he requested that they be mustered out of service. The captain was ready to return to civilian life anyway. On September 23, 1851, the Texans lined up in the plaza at Laredo for the muster-out ceremony. When they were civilians again, Ford came before them to deliver a short address: "If there is anything that endears one man to another more than having stood shoulder to shoulder in the moment of danger—I am not apprised of its existence. The tie binding soldier-comrades has its origin in the deepest recesses of the heart. But these ties, hard as it may seem, have to be broken. We must make ourselves familiar with other scenes than those transpiring in the camp and the field. We must form other associations." But above all else, "the reputation we have acquired, should be valued beyond price. I trust there is not one of us who will so act as to tarnish our good name, but that each one of us will, on the contrary, use every exertion to sustain it here and elsewhere."

V

Texas
Under
the
Secessionists

After the Texas Rangers had left the southern Río Grande country that fall of 1851, nobody was happy because in a few months renegade Comanches came back to steal horses and plunder ranches as they had done earlier. Soon Comanche bands were attacking settlements in west and north Texas, too, and pioneers all along the frontier line begged the governor for help. The governor agreed that something should be done, but the state could scarcely afford any Ranger operations at this time. Besides, he said, frontier protection was supposed to be the responsibility of the United States Cavalry. But the United States Cavalry, scattered along the river at frontier outposts, in turn insisted that it could not possibly do the job alone.

Finally, when violence on the frontier seemed out of control, the governor had no choice but to call out Ford's Rangers to help the pioneers. In 1858 the captain led an expedition against the entire Comanche nation on the Canadian River in the faraway Panhandle, scattering the Indians and burning their villages in a running, ten-hour battle. Again, in 1859–60, Ford's Rangers assisted United States Cavalry detachments under Major Sam Heintzelman and Colonel

Robert E. Lee in whipping a Mexican outlaw band under Juan Cortina which had been ravaging "gringo" settlements along the Río Grande with as much racial hatred as the Texans themselves had generated back in the Mexican War.

But volunteer companies like Ford's could not adequately police all of the state's far-flung frontiers against renegade Comanches and Mexican bandits. Only the federal government could do that, the Texans insisted. But the federal government was understandably more concerned with inflammatory events like John Brown's raid on Harper's Ferry and South Carolina's threats of secession than with distant Texas and her frontier troubles. This attitude infuriated the Texans. They also began to talk of secession. They also began to see abolitionist plots within the federal government to free their slaves; they also cried out against Northern "economic coercion." But the federal government's lackadaisical attitude toward Texas' frontier problems remained one of the chief sources of antagonism. In Rip Ford's opinion, it was ample "cause to sever . . . connection with the Union on this very head."

By the crucial summer of 1860 this was the prevailing mood in that isolated frontier state—a burning distrust of the far-off central government, a growing fear of events which Texans did not fully understand, events like the tangled controversy over Kansas and the extension of slavery into the territories, the rise of the sectional Republican party and the upsurge of abolitionism in the North, both of which the Texans associated with Negro revolution, with ravished women (first the Comanches, now the Negroes, if the "Black Republicans" got their way), with violence and destruction. Thus storm clouds were gathering along the nation's southwestern horizon too, as Texas fire-eaters threatened disunion if the Republicans won the approaching election of 1860 and took over the hated federal government.

The narrative that follows explores the reaction of Texas to Lincoln's election and attempts to portray what it was like to live in that distant state during that tragic and lamentable war.

ACROSS the United States that eventful November telegraph wires carried the crucial news: on November 6, 1860, Abraham Lincoln running on the Republican party ticket had been elected President by a largely sectional vote. South Carolina, long known as a "hotbed of agitation and nullification," cried out that the federal government, controlled by Northern Republicans, would destroy Southern institutions. On December 20, South Carolina adopted an ordinance of secession, imploring the other Southern states to do the same. As the winter days wore on, Alabama, Mississippi, and Florida cast their lots with South Carolina. Georgia and Louisiana soon joined them. The signs were ominous, and an anxious nation turned to Texas, the Lone Star State.

Linked to the slaveholding South by sentiment and belief, Texans were united in opposition to that "Black Republican," Abraham Lincoln.[1] A few days after his election, the Lone Star flag was flying over a number of Texas cities.[2]

[1] Not a Texan voted for Lincoln in the election. Only 410 votes went to Stephen A. Douglas, whom Texans considered "the bitterest pill a States Right democrat could be made to swallow." Houston *Tri-Weekly Telegraph*, April 3, 1860. John C. Breckinridge carried the state with 47,548 votes. John Bell received 15,463 votes.

[2] Secessionists flew the Lone Star flag over Galveston on November 8 and then raised it over all the major cities—Houston, Richmond, Huntsville, Gonzales, Navasota, Waco, and Dallas. O. M. Roberts to John H. Reagan, November 25, 1860, in Roberts, Papers (Archives, University of Texas Library); Francis R. Lubbock, *Six Decades in Texas*, 267–313. For a short account of the secession movement before the election, see Anna Irene Sandbo, "Beginnings of the Secession Movement in Texas," *Southwestern Historical Quarterly*, XVIII (July, 1914), 41–73. Those wanting book-length treatment which utilizes recent historical scholarship should read Earl W. Fornell, *The Galveston Era: The Texas Crescent on the Eve of Secession*.

Hotheaded secessionists were clamoring for disunion. Austin especially was a scene of feverish activity, as groups of die-hard Democrats marched up and down Congress Avenue waving torches and carrying signs condemning Lincoln and his "abolitionist" government. The secessionists, led by Oran M. Roberts, C. R. Johns, George Flournoy, and Rip Ford, broke up small Unionist meetings and denounced anyone who spoke for moderation.[3] "Me and Old Rip had like to got to fighting the other night," Unionist Aaron Burleson told his cousin on November 19, "and dam him I will whip him if he does attempt to stop me from speaking my sentiments at any place or time in these United States God dam him."[4]

"Damn the Union and Abraham Lincoln," a crowd chanted at a secession rally. On the platform Roberts and John A. Green, speaking in favor of another Texas Republic, were followed by others advocating a similar course. But over in the capitol, Governor Sam Houston, in the face of state-wide sentiment for secession, still refused to call a convention to consider it, still argued that as loyal Americans who believed in the democratic process, they must all submit to Lincoln's victory at the polls. So secessionists Roberts, Ford, Flournoy, and W. P. Rogers, ignoring law and constitution, issued their own call for a convention to assemble at Austin on January 28, 1861. Delegates were to be chosen in a special election on January 8.[5]

---

[3] Ford, *Rip Ford's Texas*, xxxv, 315–18; Oran M. Roberts' Notes on the Secession Movement, in Ford, Memoirs (Archives, University of Texas Library), V, 942–93.

[4] A. B. Burleson to Ed. Burleson (Jr.), November 19, 1860, in Burleson, Papers (Archives, University of Texas Library).

[5] An example of this call is in the *State Gazette* (Austin), December 8, 1860. See also E. W. Winkler (ed.), *Journal of the Secession Convention of Texas, 1861*, 9–12; and Roberts' Notes on the Secession Movement, in Ford, Memoirs, V, 942–93.

When word came that citizens in other towns across the state were also holding mass demonstrations by torchlight, Roberts, Ford, and others planned a large parade in Austin for January 5. At mid-morning it moved off from the capitol, with parade marshal Ford in front on a white stallion, followed by a blaring brass band, then a weaving line of carriages full of ladies who waved Lone Star flags, and finally a number of yipping political leaders and businessmen on horseback. Down Congress Avenue went the blatant demonstrators, swinging around the corner of Eighth Street and stopping at last at the intersection of Eighth and Colorado. There, while everyone shouted as loud as he could for a full ten minutes, a color guard ran the Lone Star flag up a 130-foot flagpole especially erected for the occasion.[6]

Through the next three weeks some 174 delegates from most of the state's representative districts arrived in Austin in carriages and on horseback. They joined in the almost interminable demonstrations until, on the prescribed day of January 28, they assembled in the Representative Hall in the capitol. One of their leaders recalling them take their seats wrote in later years that "lawyers of distinction, military men, farmers, merchants, physicians, preachers, were there" and were "a remarkable selection of men."[7] The first business of the day was to elect a president. As men stood up to nominate their favorites, members of the legislature who were not delegates and a crowd of "interested spectators" gathered in the galleries. Soon they heard someone announce that Judge Oran M. Roberts, a slow, methodical Austinite who spoke with a consummate drawl, had been elected president, and "quick as an electric flash" the crowd

[6] Frank Brown, "Annals of Travis County and the City of Austin from the Earliest Times to the Close of 1875" (MS, Archives, University of Texas Library), chap. 21, pp. 4–5.

[7] Oran M. Roberts, "The Political, Legislative, and Judicial History of Texas For Its Fifty Years of Statehood, 1845–1895," in *Comprehensive History of Texas*, II, 99–100.

cheered "triumphant, defiant, simultaneous," cheering "again and again with reverberations that filled the whole house."[8]

When the shouting stopped at last, the delegates got quickly down to business. Through that afternoon and those of January 29 and 30 they discussed the constitutionality of secession, justifying it by an old political philosophy—the compact theory of government, better known in 1861 as "state rights." According to this theory, the United States Constitution was a compact among free, sovereign, independent states that had originally covenanted together of their own free will and in the same manner could dissolve that union whenever the central government tried to destroy a state's independence and ancestral institutions. This argument (as the handful of antisecessionists must have pointed out) contradicted the "supreme law of the land" clause in Article VI of the Constitution. But Texas secessionists, like their counterparts east of the Sabine, cheerfully ignored this clause and underscored the Tenth Amendment, which gave to the states those powers not specifically delegated to the national government and thus, the secessionists argued, guaranteed the states the right to secede. Only Rip Ford and a few other disunionists admitted that this argument was untenable, since the "supreme law of the land" was a power specifically given to the national government and therefore could not be a residual power of the states. But if Ford did not believe in the constitutionality of secession, he did believe in the right of revolution, and that, he told his fellow delegates, was how Texas should finally justify her course.[9]

Most of the others, though, clung obdurately to the state rights argument, and on February 1, by a vote of 166 to 8, the convention adopted a secession ordinance declaring that

[8] *Ibid.*, 100.
[9] Ford, *Rip Ford's Texas*, xxxvi.

Texas "is a separate Sovereign State; and that her citizens and people are absolved from all allegiances to the United States or the government thereof." The convention sumitted the ordinance to the voters, who would ratify it in a special election on February 23, and then proceeded to draw up a declaration of causes showing why Texas was impelled to secede. The central government, the Texans insisted, had violated the original compact of union in a number of ways. Chief among them was the fact that the government had failed miserably to provide adequate protection for settlers living on the Texas frontier. Furthermore, "the recent developments in Federal affairs"—the North's attempts to exclude slavery from western territories, the civil war in Kansas which Texans believed the abolitionists had started and which the "imbecility" of the federal government had allowed to go unchecked (the Texans were now unleashing all their pent-up hatred of the federal government which had been mounting since the Snively Expedition), the rise of "Northern fanatics and extremists" in Washington—"make it evident that the power of the Federal government is sought to be made a weapon with which to strike down the interests and prosperity of the people of Texas and her sister slave-holding States, instead of permitting it to be, as was intended, our shield against outrage and aggression." How lamentable, the Texans cried, that the North was so hostile to the "Southern States and their beneficent and patriarchal system of African slavery." How unnatural that the North should proclaim "the debasing doctrine of the equality of all men, irrespective of race or color—a doctrine at war with nature, in opposition to the experience of mankind, and in violation of the plainest revelations of the Divine Law."

Ignoring the passion for equality that had been a moving force in the founding of the nation, the Texas delegates justified their pretext for disunion in self-righteous and then in pious terms: "We hold as undeniable truths that the governments of the various States, and of the confederacy itself, were established exclusively by the white race, for themselves and their posterity; that the African race had no agency in their establishment; that they were rightfully held and regarded as an inferior and dependent race, and in that condition only could their existence in this country be rendered beneficial or tolerable.

"That in this free government *all white men are and of right ought to be entitled to equal civil and political rights*; that the servitude of the African race, as existing in these States, is mutually beneficial to both bond and free, and is abundantly authorized and justified by the experience of mankind, and the revealed will of the Almighty Creator, as recognized by all Christian nations; while the destruction of the existing relations between the two races, as advocated by our sectional enemies, would bring inevitable calamities upon both and desolation upon the fifteen slaveholding States."[10]

The convention adjourned on February 4 to await the vote. On election day the ordinance passed by an impressive margin, 46,129 to 14,697, and the convention reassembled on March 2 to announce the returns and to pass an ordinance uniting Texas to the newly formed Confederate States of America.[11]

In almost every town across the state Texans cheered and danced in the streets; militia units paraded noisily; cannon boomed. The sovereign state of Texas was once again free of the tyranny of the federal government and everywhere there was a feeling of buoyant optimism. Few thought violence would come. The Republicans surely would not risk a

[10] Winkler, *Journal of the Secession Convention*, 47–49, 61–66. See also Anna Irene Sandbo, "First Session of the Secession Convention in Texas," *Southwestern Historical Quarterly*, XVIII (October, 1914), 162–94.

[11] Winkler, *Journal of the Secession Convention*, 88–97.

fight with the "blood-and-thunder men of the South." Most felt that Northerners were cowards anyway, and one man suggested facetiously that Southerners should "set out an immense trotline, bait the fish hooks with postage stamps, and 'catch all the Yankees.' "[12] To Texans that stormy winter, war was distant, war was unreal.

While citizens were rejoicing, the reassembled convention was busily setting up the political machinery for Confederate Texas. On March 14 the delegates adopted an ordinance maintaining the present state government whose officials, to stay in office, had to declare their allegiance to the Confederacy.[13] Governor Houston, who believed secession was treason, refused to take the oath. A Presbyterian minister, present at the convention, recalled that "the officer of the gathering up stairs summoned the old man three times to come forward and take the oath of allegiance. . . . I remember as yesterday the call thrice repeated—'Sam Houston! Sam Houston! Sam Houston!' but the man sat silent, immovable, in his chair below, whittling steadily on."[14] Still, because he loved Texas "too well to bring civil strife and bloodshed upon her," Houston rejected President Lincoln's proposal to help him oppose the secessionists with force and withdrew from his office peacefully.[15] The convention promptly gave Lieutenant Governor Edward Clark the governorship, and Houston, humiliated and embittered, retired to his farm near Huntsville, remaining a loyal Unionist until his death on July 26, 1863.[16]

[12] Ford, *Rip Ford's Texas*, 316.

[13] Winkler, *Journal of the Secession Convention*, 178–79.

[14] William Mumford Baker, "A Pivotal Point," *Lippincott's Magazine*, XXVI (November, 1880), 566.

[15] See Llerena Friend, *Sam Houston, the Great Designer*, 339–42.

[16] Houston withdrew from office knowing with fear in his heart that "the time has come when a man's section is his country." After war began in April, he said that while he remained a confirmed Unionist he would not fight against the Confederacy. "All my hopes, my fortunes, are centered in the South. When I see the land for whose defence my blood has been spilt, and the

Most of the other state officers took the oath; the convention, its work done, then adjourned *sine die* on March 26; and Texans moved with alacrity into what they considered a new experiment in nationhood. The legislature met briefly to designate an election for Confederate congressmen and to adopt constitutional amendments—one gave Texas the right to secede, the others related to "internal matters"—and then adjourned so that its members could volunteer in "The Army of Texas." After that, political matters "sank into comparative insignificance" as Texas leaders vied with one another to get military commands. There were no conventions, no political parties except the Democratic, and no choice in elections among issues or ideologies. Men like Francis R. Lubbock and Pendleton Murrah, the war governors after Clark, defeated their political opponents mainly because they were more convincing in their promises to prosecute the war with unyielding determination. From April, 1861, on, said Judge Roberts, who himself took the field at the head of an infantry regiment, "both the people and the government" absorbed themselves "in measures relating to military operations."[17]

The agency in charge of such operations was a fifteen-man Committee of Public Safety whose members all had military experience. The secession convention had set it up

people whose fortunes have been mine through a quarter century of toil, threatened with invasion, I can but cast my lot with theirs and await the issue." As he waited, he was plagued with illness and, some said, with senility. Arthur Fremantle, the English traveler, saw him in Galveston in May, 1863—only two months before his death—and recorded that "though evidently a remarkable and clever man, he is extremely egotistical and vain and much disappointed at having to subside from his former grandeur. . . . In appearance he is a tall, handsome old man, much given to chewing tobacco, and blowing his nose with his fingers." Houston's speech at Independence, May 10, 1861, in *The Writings of Sam Houston* (ed. Amelia W. Williams and Eugene C. Barker), VIII, 405; Arthur James Lyon Fremantle, *The Fremantle Diary* (ed. Walter Lord), 53–54.

[17] Roberts, "The Political, Legislative, and Judicial History of Texas For Its Fifty Years of Statehood, 1845–1895," in *Comprehensive History of Texas*, II, 133, 142.

back on January 30 to raise a state army with which to fight the Federals and ensure the safety of citizens until the Confederate Army should become effective in Texas. The committee had then named the McCulloch brothers—Ben and Henry—and Rip Ford colonels of cavalry in the Army of Texas. They had orders to recruit volunteer cavalry regiments and capture all Union forts and munitions of war for the state.[18]

On the night of February 15, Ben McCulloch, the Texas Ranger who had led the charge on the Bishop's Palace at Monterrey during the Mexican War and who had had a brief career as a California forty-niner and sheriff of Sacramento County, secretly assembled a thousand volunteers on Cibolo Creek near San Antonio. Their objective was the historic Alamo, then a United States fort under the command of General David E. Twiggs. The next day at dawn, Colonel McCulloch, wearing a striking "uniform" of black velvet, led his Texans into town. They occupied the roofs of buildings surrounding the Alamo and, through their gun sights, drew beads on army sentries barely visible on the distant ramparts. Inside the Alamo, the soldiers who saw the Texans' blurred figures decided that to fight them was hopeless and surrendered to McCulloch without a shot having been fired.[19]

The Texans were ecstatic. At the Grand Plaza later that day they celebrated their victory—for the South it was the first victory west of the Mississippi, won some two months before Fort Sumter and the opening of the Civil War. The celebration soon became a dazzling fiesta in which the Texans drank free liquor and ate free food—gifts from happy

[18] Winkler, *Journal of the Secession Convention*, 24, 28, 264, 309, 317–19, 320–24, 366–68.

[19] D. E. Twiggs to C. L. Thomas, February 19, 1861, in U.S. War Department, *The War of the Rebellion: A Compilation of the Official Records of the Union and Confederate Armies*, ser. I, vol. I, 504 (Hereafter referred to as *Official Records*).

civilians who exactly one week later would vote in favor of secession—and danced with "beautiful señoras" to guitar and song of the caballeros. The volunteers regrouped later in the evening to cheer and wave their rifles overhead as their commander and other well-known men gave talks about the glory of Texas and the South.[20]

When official agents of the state took charge of the Alamo on February 19, the volunteers whose services were no longer needed disbanded and went home in groups and individually. Many of them, including Ben McCulloch, would join the Confederate Army in the months that followed.[21]

The next day, February 20, Henry E. McCulloch's regiment assembled in the Alamo City and prepared to ride north. Unlike his dashing brother, Henry was a taciturn, unassuming man, but he was a reliable cavalry officer and quite popular with his troops. That evening, as civilians again gathered in the streets to watch, Henry McCulloch's riders trotted through town and headed across mesquite country toward the Red River. Through the next month the outfit captured Camp Colorado, Fort Chadbourne, Camp Cooper, and Fort Belknap. Colonel McCulloch soon got a Confederate commission and rode back to San Antonio to recruit additional companies for his cavalry regiment. On April 15, 1861, ten full companies from Bexar, Travis, Gonzales, and surrounding counties organized as the 1st McCulloch Texas Mounted Rifles—the first military outfit from Texas to enter the Confederate Army.[22]

While Henry McCulloch worked in San Antonio, Rip

[20] Caroline B. Darrow, "Recollections of the Twiggs Surrender," in Robert V. Johnson and Clarence C. Buel (eds.), *Battles and Leaders of the Civil War*, I, 33–39; San Antonio *Herald*, February 23, 1861.

[21] J. K. P. Blackburn, "Reminiscences of the Terry Rangers," *Southwestern Historical Quarterly*, XXII (July and October, 1918), 38–39.

[22] Edward Clark to Jefferson Davis, April 4, 1861, *Official Records*, ser. I, vol. I, 621; "Texas and Texans in the Civil War, 1861–1865," in *Comprehensive History of Texas*, II, 573–74.

Ford rode around the Houston area signing up recruits. On February 20, some five hundred eager volunteers reported for duty at Ford's Houston headquarters. The next day the colonel marched them over to Galveston, where they boarded the schooner *Shark* and the steamer *General Rusk* and sailed down the coast to an amphibious landing at Brazos Island, a United States stronghold a few miles up the coast from Brownsville. The island's twelve defenders surrendered almost at once. After locking them in the stockade, the Texans beat the brush over the island looking for men who might have fled during the landing. Then the horsemen reassembled on the parade grounds to hear Colonel Ford warn them not to shoot an enemy soldier except in self defense, for the colonel had orders to avoid violence if at all possible. The Texans agreed, but grudgingly. They stood there in silence as a color guard ran the Lone Star flag up the pole while cannon boomed.[23]

On February 23, Ford and his staff went onto the mainland for a talk with the Union commander at Fort Brown. The talk consumed many days; winter turned to spring; back on Brazos Island the Texans, spoiling for a fight, began taking pot shots at flying birds or thrown rocks and sticks. On March 4 they sent Colonel Ford an angry note. That morning, the note said, the Texans had heard "the explosion of guns" in the direction of Fort Brown. Later they learned that the noise was nothing less than a Federal salute honoring Lincoln's inauguration. The Texans were outraged, the note continued, and were going down to Fort Brown "and avenge the insult offered to Texas." Ford knew the temperament of his volunteers well enough to believe them. He told the Federal commander what was in the air. The two officers quite soon reached an understanding, and Rip Ford on

[23] Ford, *Rip Ford's Texas*, 318–20; Ford to J. C. Robertson, February 22 and 25, 1861, *Official Records*, ser. I, vol. LIII, 651–52, 655.

March 20 publicly announced the capture of all United States forts from Brownsville out to El Paso.[24] Through the next month his hard-boiled Texans stood guard in the lower Río Grande country as United States troops boarded their ships and sailed away to less hostile parts. On April 18, Ford lined his men up in Fort Brown and congratulated them for their bloodless victory and talked eloquently about their new nation born not of war, but of peace and a vision of destiny. That afternoon the news of Fort Sumter arrived.[25]

The Texans were happy about it. Now they could shoot the next Federals they encountered. After they were sworn into Confederate service as the 2nd Texas Cavalry, they occupied the outposts along the Great River. During the next two years they spent most of their time in the saddle, fighting small bands of Union cavalry, renegade Comanches, and Mexican outlaws led by Colonel Ford's old enemy, Juan "Cheno" Cortina, whose army of bandits had terrorized the border country in the so-called Cortina War back in 1859 and 1860. The cavalry chased Cortina up and down Webb County, fought several of his detachments in wild running battles, and finally drove the Mexicans across the border. Except for scattered Comanche raids, the river people then enjoyed a brief period of peace.[26]

While his cavalry patrolled the border, Colonel Ford himself remained in Brownsville. Since Federal troops had gone, the town was almost without law and order. Gunmen and drunks roamed the streets and brawled in saloons. The military police who soon garrisoned the town under Ford's orders were not altogether successful, for in 1863, Arthur Fremantle found Brownsville still "the rowdiest town of

[24] Ford, *Rip Ford's Texas*, 320. For the documents relating to the surrender of Federal forts along the Río Grande, see *Official Records*, ser. I, vol. LIII, 618–66.

[25] Ford, *Rip Ford's Texas*, 320–25.

[26] Stephen B. Oates, "John S. 'Rip' Ford: Prudent Cavalryman, C.S.A.," *Southwestern Historical Quarterly*, LXIV (January, 1961), 293–95.

Texas," which was "the most lawless state in the Confederacy." In Brownsville "the shooting-down and stringing-up systems are much in vogue."[27]

Colonel Ford did all he could to maintain order in his district and to help the Confederacy. In December, 1861, he supervised the construction of coastal defenses in the Brownsville area and in the spring of 1862 negotiated a trade agreement with the Mexicans. This agreement was extremely important to Confederate armies all over the South, since Matamoros furnished a medium for Confederate-European trade as well as a good market for the sale of cotton and the acquisition of arms and other military supplies. If it had not been for Ford's ability to deal with the Mexicans and for the cavalry patrols he detailed to guard the wagon trains that rolled back and forth across the border, the Confederate Trans-Mississippi Department might have collapsed early in the war.[28] Except for a brief tour of duty as state conscript commander, Colonel Ford would continue to do able service along the river until the end.

While Ford himself carried Confederate colors through the lower Río Grande country, Lieutenant Colonel John R. Baylor led some 250 riders up to El Paso with orders to capture United States forts along the upper Río Grande. In July, 1861, Baylor's column took Fort Bliss, then turned north and followed the river up to Fort Fillmore, some forty miles to the north. As the Texans approached, they heard shouts of men and roll of drums inside the fort; deciding not to attack, the invaders forded the river and occupied the village of Mesilla, whose inhabitants received them with "vivas and hurrahs." The Texans had barely dismounted when they saw, across the river, a column of Federal cavalry

---

[27] Fremantle, *The Fremantle Diary*, 10, 17–18; Ford, *Rip Ford's Texas*, 327n.

[28] Ford, *Rip Ford's Texas*, xxxvii; Oran M. Roberts, "Texas," in *Confederate Military History* (ed. Clement A. Evans), XI, 54.

approaching in the sandy haze of that sweltering July afternoon. The Texans scrambled for positions; soon a respectable skirmish was under way as the opposing forces peppered away at each other. Then, inexplicably, the Federals withdrew. Confederates pursued them, cautiously, and slept that night within view of the fort. The next morning they found it deserted, but discovered wagon tracks moving off toward the distant rim of the plains, and set out to find the enemy troops. After a harrowing ride over the blowing sand, following a dim trail that veered to the north onto the high plains east of the river, the Texans at last overtook the Union column, including women and children and a variety of wagons, at San Augustine Springs. The Federals, who were lying on the ground "almost dead from fatigue and thirst," surrendered without a fight. A few days later, on August 1, Baylor issued a proclamation claiming southern New Mexico and all of Arizona as a Confederate territory, with Mesilla as its capital and Baylor as its governor.[29]

Baylor's force was merely the advance of a larger Texan invasion designed to capture the entire Far West, to bring into the Confederacy the vast mountain ranges from Denver to California, the ports all along the Pacific coast, Arizona, New Mexico, and—either by military occupation or purchase—Baja California, Sonora, and Chihuahua. This was, of course, a revival of the old Texan dream of westward expansion and continental empire, only this time, backed by the Confederate government and Confederate money, expansionism might actually work. If so, it would not only give the Confederates a transcontinental scope with world outlets on two oceans, but would give them untold riches as

[29] For a complete account of Baylor's operations in southern New Mexico, see the Stagecoach Press's edition of Major James Cooper McKee, *Narrative of the Surrender of a Command of U.S. Forces at Fort Fillmore, New Mexico, in July, A.D. 1861, with Related Reports by John R. Baylor, C.S.A., & Others.* McKee, a Pennsylvania surgeon, tells the Federal side; Baylor relates the Confederate.

well—the gold fields in Colorado and California, which Lincoln called "the life-blood" of the Union's financial credit.[30]

The man who planned this "romantic gamble" was Henry Hopkins Sibley, a sedate, pompous brigadier who had served in the army along the Río Grande before the war and who claimed extensive knowledge of the river people and the surrounding terrain. At Richmond, Sibley outlined his plan to President Davis, who then gave him a command to be known ultimately as "The Army of New Mexico." Sibley hurried to Texas and recruited some 2,250 volunteers in August and September. The general spent another month putting his Texans through drill and giving them speeches about the riches and glory that awaited them in the West, where the sun set. Finally, on "that cold, frosty morning" of November 7, Sibley's army marched out of San Antonio singing the "Texas Ranger," as a variety of regimental and company flags whipped about in the wind overhead.[31] It was a motley crowd that moved over the road to Fort Clark that day: some on horses and others on foot, armed with bowie knives, shotguns, and rifles that varied widely in make and caliber, following their general who, jostling along in his elaborate carriage, sipped from a bottle of whisky and dreamed. Their immediate objective was to proceed up the New Mexico Río Grande, capturing forts and liberating towns like Albuquerque and Santa Fe whose inhabitants, Sibley had heard, were pro-Southern, and then to launch the grand plan, sweeping through Colorado and on across Utah to the Pacific.

Through November and into December, the column moved casually, stopping here and resting there, strutting

[30] Unless otherwise cited, the above account of the New Mexico expedition is based on Martin Hardwick Hall, *Sibley's New Mexico Campaign.*

[31] Theo. Noel, *A Campaign From Santa Fe to the Mississippi: Being a History of the Old Sibley Brigade,* 14–17.

with much pomp and noise through villages along the way to El Paso. As Christmas neared, the invaders stopped to regroup at Fort Bliss, then edged up the river to join Baylor's troops (now under Major Charles L. Pyron) at Fort Fillmore. During January, Sibley sent out detachments to capture isolated outposts and to chase down a band of Apaches that had stolen some seventy Confederate mules by moonlight. On February 3 the invasionary force advanced up river to Fort Thorn. Twelve days later it started forward again to the "quick crack and thundering report" of trump and gun.[32]

On February 20, 1862, the column passed Fort Craig on the opposite side of the river and the next day moved on to the mesa of Valverde, when "lo, and behold, an army of blue coats was seen, the first that ever met the eyes of Sibley's Brigade"—it was E.R.S. Canby's Regulars and New Mexico volunteers from Fort Craig. Suddenly there was "a jet of smoke and boom! boom! and the very air was filled with graveyard sounds" as the battle of Valverde opened, to last all day.[33] Midway in the fighting General Sibley became mysteriously "indisposed"—some said he was drunk—and field command devolved on Colonel Tom Green of the 5th Texas. Green, one of Jack Hays's Ranger captains in the Mexican War, then led his Texans in a charge that "was terrific beyond description" and drove the Federals across the river in defeat. Yet Canby would not surrender. Again and again he answered Confederate demands with a resounding no. So the Texans, as demoralized in victory as the Federals were in defeat, decided to move ahead and find action elsewhere. Their objective was the last major Federal outpost in New Mexico, Fort Union, located beyond the formidable Sangre de Cristo Range some fifty miles northeast of Santa Fe.

[32] Ibid., 24.　　　[33] Ibid., 26.

As they marched along the eastern bank of the river, the invaders were beset with hardships: food, so scarce, had to be severely rationed; the fierce February wind squalled down the river, freezing their fingers to their weapons; the wind stirred up the sand so much that they could scarcely breathe. But they marched on, somehow, over that cold brooding land, their dreams dead in their minds, their bodies aching from hunger and from a terrible fever. Many of them collapsed in the sand, left there to be eaten by carnivorous animals or to freeze as the column pushed relentlessly on. It captured Albuquerque without a fight in early March. Colonel Green then took the Confederate main body into the mountains where water was fresh and game plentiful; General Sibley remained in town to drink in private and, ostensibly, to make plans.

On March 18, the general sent Major Pyron with eighty men up to Santa Fe; it, too, fell without a fight. While there Pyron heard that Federals from Fort Union were marching over the mountains to drive him away. Seldom lacking in pugnacity, Pyron took his men to meet them. About four miles up Apache Canyon the Texans suddenly found Union infantry "upon the hills on both sides of us shooting us down like sheep." "Regular demons" they were, a Texan recalled, "upon whom iron and lead had no effect." They turned out to be a regiment of "Pike's Peakers" from the Colorado gold mines who had reinforced Fort Union after a brilliant march through ice and snow. The Confederates fell back out of the canyon, soundly beaten. They soon regrouped and with reinforcements came back on March 28 to renew the fighting, but Federals led by Major John Chivington, a Colorado preacher, again turned them back in a furious battle between the slopes of Glorieta Pass. For the Confederates, it was the beginning of the end. They retreated back to Santa

Fe where they met Colonel Green coming up fast with the rest of the army. The combined forces then rode south to join Sibley at Albuquerque. That evening a lone Confederate scout rode into town bearing ominous news: Canby with a reorganized force was marching up from Fort Craig. On April 8, Canby reached Albuquerque, exchanged artillery salvos with the Texans, then retired into the mountains to wait for Chivington.

Caught between two superior Union forces, the Texans decided to get out while they still could and headed down the river on April 12. Fortunately for them, the Federal pursuit was anything but prompt and vigorous. Was it because Canby was alleged to be Sibley's brother-in-law? men in both armies wondered. Or was Canby going to let nature do his job for him? For the Texans, demoralized and exhausted, were retreating over a merciless desert without medicine or food. Somehow, though, they made it over that vicious land and in the late spring of 1862 came at last to Fort Bliss, having sustained some 1,000 casualties on a campaign that began as a dream of glory and ended as a dark, foreboding nightmare. Sibley himself, in the face of a vengeful "public clamor raised against him," told the Richmond government "that, except for its geographical position, the Territory of New Mexico is not worth a quarter of the blood and treasure expended on its conquest. . . . I cannot speak encouragingly for the future, my troops, having manifested a dogged, irreconcilable detestation of the country and its people."[34] Thus ended once and for all Confederate hopes and Texan dreams of a transcontinental empire.

And thus ended General Sibley's career as a reputable field commander. He led his brigade, after it reorganized, for a few months and then saw only limited service in Louisi-

[34] Sibley's report, May 4, 1862, *Official Records*, ser. I, vol. IX, 509–12.

ana and Arkansas, mainly as a commander of baggage trains or as a staff officer under Generals Richard Taylor and E. Kirby Smith.

The Sibley Brigade, though, saw considerable action in the years that followed. That November it reorganized as a new command, first under Sibley and then under Tom "Daddy" Green, who came back from New Mexico with a reputation as a fighting officer. Part of the brigade under Green himself went on to fight in the battle of Galveston, and the entire outfit then joined Richard Taylor's army in Louisiana to fight in the Lafourche-Teche and Red River campaigns. In the Red River operations, Green, then a major general, led a regrettable attack against Federal gunboats and fell with his head torn away by grapeshot. His death caused the Texans, who believed "Daddy" the best and most popular cavalryman in the army, to shed "many a tear" and even moved one hard-bitten young veteran to write: "But greater sorrow cannot find a place, Than for our Green, the bravest of our race."[35]

On its way to and from New Mexico, the Sibley Brigade passed through the lower frontier region between Fort Clark and Fort Duncan on the Río Grande. As they marched, the troops no doubt heard the settlers there tell harrowing tales about Indian raids and Indian savagery. Neither federal nor state governments had ever given them adequate protection; once civil war began, pioneers living all along the frontier line—a line that extended from Fort Clark northward to the Cross Timbers and Forth Worth, then on to the Red River— knew violence beyond their memory. For news of civil war sent Federal garrisons fleeing for their lives to Kansas, and the same news brought Comanche warriors riding down off the Staked Plains to pillage and burn the white man's homesteads, killing and scalping with a vengeance. On through

[35] Noel, *A Campaign From Santa Fe to the Mississippi*, 124.

the spring of 1861, as Texas secessionists looked to the east toward Sumter or to the west toward empire, renegade Comanches ravaged their frontier with lance and fire.[36]

Settlers who survived the raids implored the government to do something, anything, to protect them. Governor Clark listened to their pleas with much sympathy; already Henry E. McCulloch had led a force into the Red River country, but, because he wanted a Confederate commission, McCulloch had gone there to capture forts rather than fight Indians. Finally, late in March, while McCulloch himself was back in San Antonio with his commission, the governor called for special volunteers to put down the pagan uprisings.[37] The Ranger companies that answered his call constituted some of the fiercest, though least trained, fighting groups Texas mustered during the war.

One of the first companies to organize was the formidable W. P. Lane Rangers of Marshall. On muster day, a member of the outfit recalled, "at an early hour the hitherto quiet of Marshall is disturbed by the 'Neigh of the war horse,' and the assembling of the cavalry" as men with beards, with revolvers and bowie knives, rode in from nearby counties. The next day over a hundred citizens turned out to witness the departure ceremonies. A group of ladies soon gathered on the courthouse lawn and prepared to present a beautiful silk flag to the company. Presently, the Lane Rangers, who had named themselves in honor of Walter P. Lane, a veteran of the Texas Revolution and the Mexican War, came riding down the main street to the courthouse, where they executed a flashy military halt in front of the circle of distinguished citizens. The troopers dismounted to stand "under arms" while Captain Sam Richardson, wearing leopard-skin pants

[36] San Antonio *Herald*, March 2, 1861; Belton *Democrat*, March 8, 1861; *Texas State Gazette* (Austin), March 16, 1861.

[37] Texas Governor, March 16–November 7, 1861 (Edward Clark), *Governor's Message: Executive Office, Austin, March 29, 1861*, 5.

and holding a double-barreled shotgun in one hand, took the
flag from one of the fair young women. At once the crowd
cheered and cheered again. Then Captain Richardson gave
an impromptu speech about Texan valor which made the
ladies weep. As they looked on, still weeping, the Rangers
mounted their horses and rode out of town that April morning "going out Indian hunting in the far west."[38]

The Lane Rangers had been in the saddle almost two
weeks when William C. Young, a federal marshal before
the war, mustered a second crack cavalry outfit for frontier
service up in Sherman, in Grayson County. Young had over
a thousand men who agreed to join the Confederate service
as the 11th Texas Cavalry but who refused to train by the
books. They trained instead by holding shooting matches
and riding tournaments, with plenty of song and women and
whisky.[39] Yet, when they rode into the Indian Territory that
June, they proved themselves a potent fighting force: they
drove away the Comanche bands operating along the Red
River, then raised the Confederate colors over Fort Ar-
buckle, Fort Washita, and Fort Cobb. The settlers praised
them. So did generals in faraway Richmond who believed
them an extremely effective cavalry outfit. As a reward for
able work, the Confederate War Department in April, 1862,
transferred the regiment to Mississippi to fight in Joseph
Wheeler's cavalry corps.[40]

The troopers were happy about the transfer, but the settlers were not; as the cavalry rode out of the frontier, the
Comanches rode back into it to loot and scalp as they had

[38] The Lane Rangers went on to become a part of Ford's Second Texas
Cavalry and to serve along the lower frontier line. William W. Heartsill, *Fourteen Hundred and Ninety-One Days in the Confederate Army; or, Camp Life,
Day by Day, of the W.P. Lane Rangers from April 19, 1861 to May 20, 1865,*
2–5 passim.

[39] Special Orders No. 18, July 25, 1861, *Official Records,* ser. I, vol. IV,
95; Dallas *Herald,* September 25, 1861.

[40] Frank W. Johnson, *A History of Texas and Texans* (ed. Eugene C.
Barker), IV, 1688; Roberts, "Texas," in *Confederate Military History,* XI, 47.

done before. Again embattled pioneers called on the governor for help, and again the governor called for volunteers, this time for a special Frontier Regiment that would serve exclusively in west Texas. This kind of service appealed to old Indian fighters who owned no slaves and who would rather fight to save their neighbors from the red man than to defend slavery and state rights. On January 29, 1862, just over a thousand Indian fighters organized in nine companies under the command of Colonel James M. Norris of Waco. That spring they occupied eighteen outposts all along the frontier line from a point on the Red River near Gainesville down to Fort Duncan on the Río Grande; Norris then left half a company at each post with orders to scout the surrounding country and shoot to kill; and for the first time that settlers could remember they had proper military protection.[41] But the Comanches did not retire altogether. Small bands remained to harass soldiers and citizens alike. Then, in 1863, they came in numbers greater than ever before to fling themselves on the isolated outposts as well as to massacre homesteaders. It was not until late 1864 that the Frontier Regiment, heavily reinforced by citizen companies, drove the hard-riding Indians back onto the Staked Plains. Even then the cavalry had to maintain a constant vigilance lest the renegades return to steal horses by moonlight. Throughout the war years and after, Texans found the Comanches their most formidable and immediate foes.[42]

On April 21, 1861, less than a month after Governor

41 Lubbock, *Six Decades in Texas*, 357.

42 Colonel Norris was a tough soldier and a martinet to his subordinates. As a result he became extremely unpopular and had to resign his post on January 10, 1863. Colonel J. E. McCord then took command and led the Frontier Regiment until the final weeks of the war. James Buckner Barry, *A Texas Ranger and Frontiersman: The Days of Buck Barry in Texas, 1845–1906* (ed. James K. Greer), 145–202; J. H. Baker, Diary (Archives, University of Texas Library); Robert Pattison Felgar, "Texas in the War for Southern Independence, 1861–1865" (Ph.D. dissertation, University of Texas, 1935), 151–68.

Clark had called out special state troops to fight the Comanches, the Confederate War Department appointed Colonel Earl Van Dorn, a West Point graduate with Mexican War service, to command the military district of Texas. He had orders to induce state troops to volunteer for Confederate service and to put the state on a thorough war footing. A congenial officer who had a respect for civilian leadership unusual among soldiers, Van Dorn soon had Governor Clark's wholehearted support. Then, with his enrolling officers, including such popular men as Ben McCulloch, the colonel traveled from camp to camp urging state troops to make the change. "Your country calls on you for further service," the Confederate officers declared; "will it call in vain? Never! We must re-enlist, or all the blood spilled is as water spilled on the ground!"[43] The Texans responded enthusiastically and by the end of May, 1861, all state troops had transferred to the Confederate service. After that, volunteers, except those who joined the Frontier Regiment, enlisted in the regular army for three years or for the war. Recruiting, especially after the draft laws became effective in the summer of 1862, was restricted to officers holding commissions in the Confederate Army, and the procedure used to recruit men was based on regulations prescribed by the War Department.[44]

Once Van Dorn had Texas preparing for hostilities, Confederate leaders made plans to defend the vast Trans-Mississippi region against an expected Federal invasion from Missouri and Kansas. On May 13, 1861, the War Department commissioned Ben McCulloch a brigadier general and sent him to Fort Smith, Arkansas, with orders to raise an

[43] Dallas *Herald*, February 5, 1862; X. B. De Bray to L. P. Walker, August 28, 1862, *Official Records*, ser. I, vol. IV, 98–100.

[44] Texas Adjutant General, *Report, November, 1861*, 1; Texas Governor, March 16–November 7, 1861 (Edward Clark), *Governor's Message to the Senators and Representatives of the Ninth Legislature of the State of Texas, November 1, 1861*, 1.

army, occupy the Indian Territory (present-day Oklahoma), then reinforce the Missouri State Guards, who were fighting desperately to hold Missouri against the Union forces.[45] McCulloch, a man of enormous energy, wasted no time in executing his orders. First of all he negotiated peace treaties with the Indian nations through their long-time friend, Albert Pike, himself a Confederate officer.[46] Then McCulloch ordered his recruiting officers throughout the Trans-Mississippi to fill out their outfits as quickly as possible and march them to Fort Smith. Among the eight regiments and two batteries that reported to McCulloch was the 3rd Texas Cavalry from Dallas.

Two men who had fighting experience as Texas Rangers, Colonel Elkanah Greer and Captain J. A. Harris, recruited the 3rd Texas among home guard companies at Rusk, Dallas, and other towns in that area. The ten companies that converged on Dallas in early June were without discipline, but were made up of pugnacious volunteers who promised to strike a blow for Texas or to perish in the attempt. Their company flags contained some names that connoted their fierceness and chauvinism. For example, Company A was the "Texas Hunters," Company C, the "Lone Star Defenders," and Company G, the "Dead Shot Rangers." After the muster-in ceremony, in which "we were subjected to no physical examination or other foolishness," the regimental bugler sounded "to horse" and the outfit left for the battle front. With ten silk flags snapping in the wind overhead, the horsemen rode through towns on the road to Fort Smith in remarkable "military style and military pomp."[47]

The 3rd Texas went on to fight under McCulloch in the

[45] S. Cooper to Ben McCulloch, May 13, 1861, *Official Records*, ser. I, vol. III, 575–76.

[46] McCulloch to L. P. Walker, June 27, September 2, 1861, *ibid.*, 595–96, 692.

[47] Samuel B. Barron, *The Lone Star Defenders: A Chronicle of the Third Texas Cavalry, Ross' Brigade*, 17–23.

battle of Wilson's Creek, Missouri, on August 10, and again at Pea Ridge, Arkansas, in March of 1862. In the Pea Ridge engagement the colorful McCulloch fell, still wearing his suit of black velvet, and so did many of the 3rd Texas. After that, the regiment crossed into Mississippi to fight under that redoubtable Louisianian, Pierre Gustave Toutant de Beauregard, and then under Braxton Bragg.[48]

So far almost all the Texas outfits raised had been cavalry. Back in April, 1861, the War Department called on the state to furnish 8,000 infantry for Confederate armies fighting in Kentucky and Virginia.[49] Governor Clark wrote back that he did not see how he could possibly get so many infantry but that he would try. He obtained commissions for prominent citizens and sent them into counties throughout the state to raise companies of foot soldiers. The recruiters soon found that Texans, well known for their peerless horsemanship, would have little to do with the infantry because they thought it unromantic and rather inglorious. Nearly every man, it seemed, wanted to join the cavalry and make a lasting impression on relatives and young ladies by riding off to war on horseback to the tune of "The Girl I Left Behind Me."[50]

Governor Clark knew then that he had to do something and soon, lest the Richmond government reprimand him for failing to send along his quota of infantry. After much thought he got a bright idea. He directed that camps of instruction be set up around the state to show the men that infantry service was every bit as glorious as that of the cavalry.[51] The results were twofold: one was that by the end of 1861, Clark's recruiters, with the help of infantry in-

---

[48] *Ibid.*, 30 ff.; Victor M. Rose, *Ross' Texas Brigade*, 18ff.

[49] L. P. Walker to Edward Clark, *Official Records*, ser. III, vol. V, 692.

[50] *Governor's Message, November 1, 1861*, 7–9.

[51] *Ibid.*; Texas Adjutant General, *Report, November, 1861*, 1; Roberts, "Texas," in *Confederate Military History*, XI, 56–57.

structors, had raised seven regiments and four battalions of foot soldiers, a total of about 7,100 men; the other was that rivalry between the two branches of the service became rather severe if not downright vicious. Cavalry and infantry recruiters vied with one another to get volunteers; generals of the respective branches quarreled and quarreled over which one was the more effective in combat; and the men themselves, wherever they met, fell to name calling and fist fighting. "Wagon dogs!" the cavalry would growl, with an air of supreme condescension. "Webfeet!" "Mud sloggers!" At that the infantry would reply, with equal malice: "There goes the buttermilk cavalry." "A hundred dollars reward for just one dead cavalryman." "All those fellows do is to find Yankees for us to kill."[52]

In terms of numbers, the cavalry of course came out the better in this rivalry. During the four years of war some 58,000 Texans joined the cavalry (though many of them were dismounted after 1862) as compared to roughly 30,000 volunteers and draftees in the infantry and artillery.[53] This was to be expected, for Texans had, after all, had a long and intimate companionship with the horse, with the six-shooter and carbine. And that these horsemen should form the back-bone of the Confederate cavalry in the Trans-Mississippi

[52] William A. Fletcher, *Rebel Private Front and Rear*, 146; *The Gray Jackets; And How They Lived, Fought, and Died, For Dixie, with Incidents and Sketches of Life in the Confederacy*, 175.

[53] This estimate is of course open to question, especially since only 92,026 Texans in 1860 were of military age (between seventeen and thirty-nine). But allowing for a slight increase in population over the next five years and considering that the army, towards the end, used men as young as fifteen and as old as fifty-five, some 110,000 Texans were potential soldiers. It seems quite likely that 88,000 of these wore the gray (Governor Lubbock put the number at 90,000) and that 22,000 were men who dodged the draft, got draft exemptions, or otherwise avoided the service. For a list of Texas cavalry outfits and a computation of the number of horsemen from Texas, see Stephen B. Oates, *Confederate Cavalry West of the River*, Appendix A and Appendix B. Lester N. Fitzhugh, *Texas Batteries, Battalions, Regiments, Commanders and Field Officers Confederate States Army, 1861–1865*, has the most accurate and complete list of infantry and artillery units.

was also to be expected. They were capable, if undisciplined, horsemen whose performances as independent raiding forces, as scouts and reconnaissance patrols for the main army, and occasionally as foot soldiers alongside the regular infantry, played a large part in keeping the Trans-Mississippi Department Confederate to the last.[54]

Texas also produced a number of highly regarded officers and outfits for Confederate armies fighting east of the Mississippi River. Perhaps the best-known officers who saw action outside the Trans-Mississippi were General Albert Sidney Johnston, who fell at Shiloh, General John B. Hood, and Colonel Benjamin Franklin Terry. Hood and Terry commanded Texan outfits that, whether on horse or on foot, fought with such ferocity that they became easily the most celebrated organizations from the state.

Terry organized his regiment of Rangers in September, 1861, in Houston. The personnel of the outfit was "of the very highest," comprising sons of prominent families, college students, merchants, lawyers, bankers, farmers, and cowboys, expert with lariat and six-shooter. Wherever they went, these Texans impressed people by their determination "to get into the war in a crack cavalry regiment."[55]

No one was more impressed than peaceful citizens of Houston. While waiting there for the order to ride, the Rangers "kept the town in a continued bustle with their daring feats of horsemanship." To "show what they could do," the men formed in squads and rode at a maddening gallop down the streets, jumping off and back on their horses and picking sticks and pieces of clothing off the ground. This apparently was not exciting enough for several men, so they rounded up some wild stallions and, yelling and firing their pistols in the air, proceeded to break them in

[54] See Stephen B. Oates, "Confederate Cavalrymen of the Trans-Mississippi," *Civil War History*, VII, 13–19.
[55] L. B. Giles, *Terry's Texas Rangers*, 13–14.

the middle of town—much to the exasperation of storekeepers who feared for their lives and property. With all this showmanship, a newspaperman decided that the Rangers, hardened from encounters with "the stealthy panther and more savage Mexican hog, in our forests," would be the "pride of Texas" and would make "the enemy beware" when they "get on their track."[56] And the Rangers did become the pride of Texas as they fought without regard for death and lost their commander and two-thirds of their numbers in engagements covering half a dozen states east of the Mississippi.[57]

Like the Rangers, Hood's Texas Brigade was a hard-fighting organization, composed of the 1st, 4th, and 5th Texas Infantry regiments. The brigade commander, John B. Hood, became the ranking Texan in the Confederate Army and toward the end of the war led the Army of Tennessee. Unfortunately for the Confederates, he led that army to near destruction at Nashville which earned him a song:

> *You may talk about your Beauregard*
> *And sing of General Lee,*
> *But the gallant Hood of Texas*
> *Played hell in Tennessee.*[58]

Confederates from other states thought him indecisive, but Texans admired the man in no uncertain terms and called him one of their own, though he was a Kentuckian by birth. He came to Texas as a young man, then went on to West Point, graduating in 1853. He served for a time in Missouri and California, then returned to Texas as a captain

[56] Houston *Tri-Weekly Telegraph*, Bellville *Countryman*, September 18, 1861.

[57] C.C. Jeffries, *Terry's Rangers*, is a eulogistic history of the Rangers (also known as the Eighth Texas Cavalry). See also Blackburn, "Reminiscences of the Terry Rangers," *Southwestern Historical Quarterly*, XXII, 38–78, 143–79; and Kate Scurry Terrell, "Terry's Texas Rangers," in *Comprehensive History of Texas*, II, 682–94.

[58] T. R. Hay, *Hood's Tennessee Campaign*, 66ff.

111

in the 2nd United States Cavalry. He remained in that capacity until war broke out, when he resigned to enter the Confederate service.[59] Good fighting earned him a colonel's commission and his own command—the 4th Texas Infantry Regiment. He soon rose to the rank of brigadier general in charge of the Texas Brigade, which became a part of James Longstreet's Corps of the Army of Northern Virginia. From then until the end of the war Hood had nothing but bad luck. At Gettysburg he received a severe wound which permanently disabled his left arm; later, at Chickamauga, he lost his left leg. After the stump healed, he returned to active duty, but for a time he was so weak that he had to be strapped to the saddle. Then came that defeat in the battle of Nashville in December, 1864, which severely damaged his reputation and caused him to resign from the army.[60]

The Texans who followed Hood in distant theaters of war were, like their fellow Confederates, rather short on military formality. When they had to attend parades, they usually displayed unmilitary notions. For example, in June, 1863, when Robert E. Lee's army gathered near Culpeper Courthouse in Virginia, Jeb Stuart's cavalry corps put on a review for the commanding general and assembled guests, including Hood's Texans. As the cavalry rode past, sabers drawn, eyes right, making a big impression on the top brass, the Texans looked on with scorn and one muttered: "Wouldn't we clean 'em out if old Hood would let us loose on 'em?"[61] Bellicose to a man, these Texans saw some of the hottest fighting in the war and sustained such heavy casualties that when they surrendered their brigade had only about

[59] Hood tells about his own military career with as much literary verve as any of his biographers. J. B. Hood, *Advance and Retreat: Personal Experiences in the United States and Confederate Armies.*

[60] See John P. Dyer, *The Gallant Hood.*

[61] John Esten Cooke, *Wearing of the Gray: Being Personal Portraits, Scenes and Adventures of the War*, 317.

557 men left out of some 4,480 initial recruits and replacements.

Once formed, Texas outfits never knew when or where they would get their meals and changes of clothing. The Richmond government could barely supply its armies in Virginia, much less those in the far-off Trans-Mississippi region; the Texas state government was equally incompetent; and the troops finally had to subsist on whatever they could get, good or bad, if they could get anything. If they had money, they bought what they needed in nearby towns; if they had no money, they stole cows, pigs, chickens, clothing, and books to read at night by fire light.[62] Probably their largest source of quartermaster stores was the countless women's committees that began to be formed around the state almost concurrently with the raising of the first regiments. These committees or ladies' aid societies collected not only blankets, socks, shoes, hats, pants, and shirts but also beef, ham, flour, salt, coffee, tea, desiccated vegetables, and candles and sent them to their men at the fighting fronts.[63] It was not until late 1863 that a quartermaster department, established in the Trans-Mississippi the year before, began to do even a fair job of supplying the troops, and even then the "uniforms" it gave out varied impossibly in color and design.[64] Arthur Fremantle, who visited with Texan troops stationed on the lower Río Grande, found that "their dress consisted simply of flannel shirts, very ancient

[62] Stephen B. Oates, "Supply for Confederate Cavalry in the Trans-Mississippi," *Military Affairs*, XXV, 94–99. Those interested in what the men themselves had to say about their hardships and how they got along might read through Heartsill, *Fourteen Hundred and Ninety-One Days*; Barron, *The Lone Star Defenders*; Joseph Blessington, *The Campaigns of Walker's Texas Division*; and John Q. Anderson, *A Texas Surgeon in the C. S. A.*

[63] Oates, *Confederate Cavalry West of the River*, 56–57.

[64] See James L. Nichols, "Confederate Quartermaster Operations in the Trans-Mississippi Department" (Master's thesis, University of Texas, 1947), 8, 20, 44–45, 123–24. Nichols' thesis has been published as *The Confederate Quartermaster in the Trans-Mississippi*.

trousers, jack boots with enormous spurs, and black felt hats ornamented with the 'Lone Star of Texas.' They looked rough and dirty."[65] Those enormous spurs in the end attracted more attention than the rest of the Texans' motley outfits. "The masses of them wore spurs on their heels," Thomas North noted, "generally the immense wheel-spur, and though they were not born with them on, yet they might as well have been, for they not only rode in them, but walked in them, ate in them, and slept in them. Their clanking as they walked was like a man in chains. They wore belts around the waist, suspended one or two revolvers and a bowie knife; were experts in the saddle, had a reckless daredevil look and were always ready for whisky and a big chew of tobacco, and the hand-writing of passion and appetite was all over them."[66]

For armament, Texas soldiers had, as Thomas North suggested, revolvers, bowie knives, muskets, shotguns, and carbines, either brought from home, purchased, stolen from peaceful civilians, or captured from the enemy.[67] The musket was the main infantry weapon; the revolver was the preferred arm for the cavalry; yet neither of these scared the enemy like those pernicious bowie knives carried by all Texan soldiers. Often three feet in length, these weapons, according to a trooper in the 3rd Texas Cavalry, were "heavy enough to cleave the skull of a mailed knight through helmet and all."[68] Another man felt that the awesome appearance of the knives "might have made a Malay's blood run cold."[69] Shotguns were popular short-range weapons for both infantry and cavalry. As a cavalryman put it, one did not have

[65] Fremantle, *The Fremantle Diary*, 7.
[66] Thomas North, *Five Years in Texas: Or, What You Did Not Hear during the War from January 1861 to January 1866*, 104.
[67] See Oates, *Confederate Cavalry West of the River*, 62–74.
[68] Rose, *Ross' Texas Brigade*, 18.
[69] Alonzo Gray, *Cavalry Tactics as Illustrated by the War of the Rebellion*, pt. I, 16.

to aim with a shotgun; and one had, moreover, a good chance of killing two, perhaps three, Federals in a single blast.[70]

Though the troops themselves furnished most of their arms, government and private firms did try to help. In May, 1862, a privately owned factory at Tyler started making a .54- and .57-caliber rifle variously called the "Texas Rifle," the "Austrian Rifle," and the "Enfield Rifle." The government bought the factory in the fall of 1863 and ran it until 1865.[71] Another private concern—Tucker, Sherrod, and Company of Lancaster—made a .44-caliber revolver called the "Tucker-Sherrod Colt Dragoon." It appeared "in every respect quite equal to the famous Colt's six shooter, of which it is an exact copy, with the exception of an extra sight on the barrel which we think is a decided improvement." The makers of this "remarkable" six-shooter intended it to be used exclusively in Texas, "as it is notorious how deficient we are in arms for home defense."[72]

The Texas government had its own plans and made efforts to manufacture arms for its troops wherever they were fighting. A government-owned arsenal at San Antonio produced small numbers of rifles, carbines, and revolvers. The Texas Military Board, set up by Governor Lubbock to purchase military supplies, had another arsenal built at Austin, which made a few cannon. Powder, cap, and cartridge for these weapons came from government factories at Austin and in Bexar County.[73]

Yet, because so many men were away in the army, these factories could find almost no one except a few women and

[70] Bellville *Countryman*, September 4, 11, 1861; Heartsill, *Fourteen Hundred and Ninety-One Days*, 50.

[71] Frank E. Vandiver, *Ploughshares into Swords: Josiah Gorgas and Confederate Ordnance*, 192.

[72] *Texas Almanac–Extra* (Austin), February 28, 1863.

[73] C. W. Ramsdell, "The Texas State Military Board, 1862–1865," *Southwestern Historical Quarterly*, XVII, 268, 272; Lubbock, *Six Decades in Texas*, 386–93.

children to work in them and so could scarcely fill the requisitions they received.[74] Texas governors therefore had to call on the Confederate Ordnance Bureau for help; Governor Lubbock on November 13, 1862, even asked for old guns that armies east of the Mississippi had discarded, if nothing else could be done.[75]

But nothing could be done, nothing at all. The Ordnance Bureau had no guns for Texas; the state government itself soon had no money left to buy or make enough to matter; and once again the men had to furnish everything themselves. By 1864, they had such difficulty in obtaining weapons, horses, food, and other necessities that they resorted more than ever to stealing them from nearby farms. The farmers of course complained angrily to the governor, describing vividly how "rough, uncivil" army bands without "responsible officers" ransacked their homes, took their flintlocks, mules, and forage and rode away swearing and shouting insults.[76] To placate the citizens, the governor did what he could: he asked officers to punish any offender they caught, then called on all Texas soldiers to respect civilians' rights and to stand by the laws of the land. Yet, the pillaging only increased, for the soldiers were hungry and poorly clad and poorly armed. It became so rampant during the last winter of hostilities that Texas citizens swore they feared their own troops more than they did the enemy.[77]

This disposition among Texan troops to steal badly needed supplies was inherent in their character, for they were not—nor had they ever been in their lives—soldiers

[74] Houston *Tri-Weekly Telegraph*, May 30, 1862; Felgar, "Texas in the War for Southern Independence," 403–406, 414.

[75] Lubbock to Davis, *Official Records*, ser. I, vol. LIII, 833–34.

[76] J. T. Harcourt to Murrah, March, 1864, Governors' Letters (Archives, Texas State Library); Jonnie M. Megee, "The Confederate Impressment Acts of the Trans-Mississippi States" (Master's thesis, University of Texas, 1915), 141.

[77] Oates, *Confederate Cavalry West of the River*, 81–82.

in the true sense of the term. They were frontiersmen who had a granite-like individualism, an open disregard for discipline, and a powerful tendency to do as they pleased, especially in times of severe privation. Like almost every Texan who had ever taken up his rifle to fight for his land and his beliefs, Texas Confederates never adjusted to the strict enforcement of orders, the gap between officers and men, the heel clicking and spit and polish so characteristic of the professional military. According to Major General Richard Taylor, Texans "had no more conception of military gradations than of the celestial hierarchy of the poets."[78]

Because of their aversion to "military gradations," because they would respect an officer only when he proved a better fighter than the men he led, Texans took a long, critical, and often disapproving look at the officers sent across the Sabine River to command the district of Texas. They grew to like Earl Van Dorn, who was there from April to September 4, 1861, because Van Dorn was a splendid horseman, an enviable fist-fighter, and a good shot with a six-shooter. Tall, wiry, and stern of voice, he knew no fear, which made him irresistibly appealing to the Texans. Besides, he respected their individualistic nature. Here was the kind of leader they would follow to their deaths. But the War Department, realizing his potential, promoted him to brigadier general with a field command in Virginia and later sent him back to head the Trans-Mississippi Department.[79]

Van Dorn's replacement, General Paul Octave Hébert, transferred in from Louisiana, was a superb example of the type of officer Texans despised. No sooner had he assumed command than he declared the entire state under martial

---

[78] Richard Taylor, *Destruction and Reconstruction: Personal Experiences in the Late War*, 150.

[79] Allen Johnson and Dumas Malone (eds.), *Dictionary of American Biography*, XIX, 492–93. See also U. S. War Department, *Memorandum Relative to the General Officers . . . of the Confederate States, 1861–1865*.

law. He issued orders, decrees, and proclamations; he demanded that the governor and other civil officers pay him homage; he ordered Texan troops to learn how to drill and parade and to study books on tactics and on military protocol. He wanted a single-line chain of command going from himself down through everyone, including civilians. A graduate of West Point (first in the class of 1840) and an assistant professor of engineering there for a year, Hébert wanted a model military district as prescribed in his books and as outlined in his notes and lectures.[80] He could not have picked a worse place than Texas to try it. Still, the Texans might have forgiven him for his administrative compulsions had he proved a fierce and gallant field commander. What they found most repulsive about him was the fact that he was "a man of no military force or practical genius" who "preferred red-top boots, and a greased rat-tail moustache, with a fine equipage, and a suit of waiters, to the use of good, practical common sense." Because they abhorred his "European red-tapeism" and because they suspected him of cowardice, the Texans became tired and disgusted with him and began to complain. They wanted a man to command them who liked to fight.[81]

Largely because of his unpopularity, the War Department removed Hébert from command on October 10, 1862, and finally, after some vacillation, transferred him into Louisiana to command the northern subdistrict. The officer who replaced him, though, seemed precisely the kind that "best suited Texas." His name was John Bankhead Magruder, and he was a tough, rugged man who could swear and drink and

[80] William Pitt Ballinger, Diaries (Archives, University of Texas Library), February–November, 1862, pp. 38–43; U.S. War Department, Service Record of Paul Octave Hébert (Confederate Records, National Archives, Washington, D.C.); John Dimitry, "Louisiana," in *Confederate Military History*, X, 307–308; *Dictionary of American Biography*, VIII, 492–93.

[81] North, *Five Years in Texas*, 105–106, 107; Lubbock, *Six Decades in Texas*, 424.

fight as effectively as any other officer the Texans had seen. He too was a West Pointer, yet he commanded not from books but from long experience as a combat officer in the Comanche wars in Texas and in the Seminole and Mexican wars. Though he carried a reputation as being "restless and hot tempered," young warriors like Thomas Jackson had requested to serve under him because "if any fighting was to be done Magruder would be 'on hand.' " Magruder knew how to entertain as well as he knew how to fight; on duty in Rhode Island before the Civil War he entertained with such courtly bearing and such a "brilliant ability to bring appearances up to the necessity of the occasion" that he got a nickname, "Prince John," and most everyone in Texas soon agreed that it was rather appropriate. Still, at bottom he was an aggressive soldier who won the respect and loyalty of his Texas troops. As a popular saying went among them, "the advent of General Magruder was equal to the addition of 50,000 men to the forces of Texas."[82]

Magruder was, however, less successful in his dealings with the civilians. As Hébert had done, Magruder ignored the Anglo-American tradition of civil over military authority that prevailed in Texas and tried to make the state, "as it were, a great military camp, subject to military rules."[83] He permitted his subdistrict commanders to rule with dictatorial powers: they suspended *habeas corpus* at their own discretion; they drew up impressment schedules which allowed soldiers to take cotton and weapons and horses and other supplies from civilians without proper compensation; and they imprisoned anyone who refused to co-operate with them. Neither Magruder nor his officers (though some of them, like Hamilton P. Bee and Henry E. McCulloch, were

[82] *Dictionary of American Biography*, XII, 204–205; Ford, *Rip Ford's Texas*, 343; North, *Five Years in Texas*, 105.

[83] Roberts, "The Political, Legislative, and Judicial History of Texas," in *Comprehensive History of Texas*, II, 145.

old Texans) really understood or appreciated the Texans' character and attitude: their peculiar individualism, their open disregard for military rankings, their opposition to military rule, and their hostility to anyone who was not a Texan infringing upon their rights.

Magruder made his most serious mistake, according to civilian leaders, when in the spring of 1864 he tried to send troops stationed in Texas for home guard purposes into Louisiana, where Confederates desperately needed men to stop a Federal invasion up the Red River. This was too much for the civil officials. Governor Murrah argued that Texas would not be stripped of her defenses and ordered the troops to stay where they were. His stand against the military brought from other politicians an outburst of criticism and denunciation of Magruder's policies. The legislature adopted a number of acts and resolutions accusing him of trying to run Texas like a despot. An example was the act of November 14, 1864, which, after impugning Magruder, made it a penal offense for military officers to refuse a prisoner the right to counsel and a just trial.[84] This act, said the chief justice of the Texas Supreme Court, "indicates the extremity to which arbitrary military power had been stretched." The court itself, in the famous *habeas corpus* case in March, 1864, restored civil rights to several subdistricts and "severely condemned" Magruder's "military assumption of power." Yet, in all fairness to Magruder, many civil officials admitted that much of this conflict arose less from his efforts to usurp power than from the absence of any clear dividing line between civil and military authority.[85]

Magruder also came under fire for his strict enforcement

[84] Texas Senate Journal, 10th Leg., 2d called sess., October 17–November 14, 1864 (MS, Archives, Texas State Library). See also resolutions of May 27, 28, 1864, remonstrating against unfair military impressment schedules, in Texas Senate Journal, 10th Leg., 1st called sess., May 9–May 28, 1864 (MS, Archives, Texas State Library).

[85] Roberts, "The Political, Legislative, and Judicial History of Texas," in

of the draft. When he took command in November, 1862, he found that Texans refused to take it seriously. Rip Ford, the state conscript commander since June 2, 1862, openly called the draft law "an unfortunate enactment" because of its unfair list of exemptions and did what any "right minded man" would. He exempted "the ferryman" and drafted "the owner of the ferry"; he exempted "the overseer of Negroes" and conscripted "the owner"—and "so on through the different kinds of employers and employees." Magruder, when he discovered what Ford was doing, promptly ordered the colonel to carry out the law as it appeared on the books. With much distaste, Ford then exempted the man of means because he owned so many slaves or so many acres of land and conscripted the poor man who owned nothing and who frequently met enrolling officers with loaded musket and cries of "Rich Man's War, Poor Man's Fight!"[86]

Texas politicians also cried out, but for a different reason. They called the draft a "remarkable" piece of legislation because it compelled Texans to fight. And no distant government, they declared, had the right or the power to *compel* Texans to do anything. In a public message Governor Murrah denounced it as unfair and unconstitutional, because it stripped Texas "of the officers provided for its administration by the . . . laws." The Texas Supreme Court, however, upheld the draft laws in a controversial decision which, according to a dissenting judge, permitted General Magruder to force into the army "the great body of the citizens of the State" who fell between the ages of seventeen and forty-six.[87]

Comprehensive History of Texas, II, 145. For an excellent evaluation of Magruder, see Ballinger, Diaries, 1862–64, p. 144.

[86] Ford, *Rip Ford's Texas*, 332–33; John S. Ford, Superintendent of Conscripts, Special Instructions to Enrolling Officers, June 25, 1862, broadside in Roberts Papers (Archives, University of Texas Library).

[87] Roberts, "The Political, Legislative, and Judicial History of Texas," in *Comprehensive History of Texas*, II, 144–46. See also the chapter on Texas in

Magruder's vigorous use of the draft had serious reper-
cussions. For one thing it caused a sharp rise in the number
of desertions in 1863 and 1864. Poor men who had been
taken away from their families soon got letters telling how
hard things were at home—the children hungry, the crops
dead in the fields, the future ominous. Forced to defend a
cause they did not understand or did not believe in, many of
these men—so condescendingly referred to among the rich
who were draft exempt as "poor white trash" or "clay eat-
ers"—set out for home on stolen horses or somehow got
furloughs and did not report back to duty.[88] It was of course
Magruder's job to arrest them. When he ordered Ford and
the subdistrict commanders to do so, deserters, rather than
go to jail, promptly joined forces with armed bands of draft
dodgers and defied Confederate authority. Several of these
bands hid out in the "Big Thicket" in Hardin County, skirmishing with Confederate detachments in the swampy waste-
lands around "Deserter's Island," "The Big Hole," and
"Panther's Den."[89] Such bands gave Rip Ford considerable
trouble in Travis County, where they shot at his enrolling
officers and terrorized the homes of loyal Confederate families. These men—Ford called them "jayhawkers"—waged
a kind of irregular war behind the lines until the Confederacy fell.[90]

Armed bodies of draft dodgers, of deserters and Unionists, also harassed Henry E. McCulloch's troops in Wise,
Denton, and other counties up in the northern subdistrict.

Margaret N. Goodlet, "The Enforcement of the Confederate Conscription
Acts in the Trans-Mississippi Department" (Master's thesis, University of
Texas, 1914).

[88] Ford, *Rip Ford's Texas*, 334–47; Houston *Tri-Weekly Telegraph*, January 19, 1863, *passim*; *Texas Almanac–Extra* (Austin), March 17, 1863.

[89] T. C. Richardson, *East Texas: Its History and Its Makers*, III, 961.

[90] Ford, *Rip Ford's Texas*, 337–38; Ford to Edmund P. Turner, July 22,
1863, *Official Records*, ser. I, vol. XXVI, pt. 2, p. 119.

Confederates should have expected this, for a majority of north Texans, whose opinions resembled those of men in the border states, had opposed the secession movement from the start and had voted against the secession ordinance. They sided with the Confederacy only after war actually began. Things were relatively quiet in north Texas until district officers in the summer of 1862 began enforcing the conscript act passed that April. For the most part, men there reacted violently to it; a number of them went so far as to organize a peace plot designed in the main to take their area out of the war. When Confederate authorities uncovered the plot that fall, they hanged some sixty-five men suspected of being involved in it and declared martial law in Cooke County, where anti-Confederate sentiment seemed the strongest. These unhappy events precipitated a veritable reign of terror in which numbers of innocent men were beaten and jailed or hanged. Others fled into the brush, where they fought off troops sent to capture them. After that, dissension spread rapidly as more and more citizens began openly to defy Confederate rule. During the winter of 1863–64, violence was so rampant in counties along the Red River that General McCulloch lamented, "The question is whether they or we shall control." Throughout that final year, officers there insisted that unless Magruder sent them reinforcements to uphold the laws, north Texas would be lost to the Confederacy.[91]

The draft law also provoked Unionist sympathizers in the Fredericksburg–San Antonio area into open resistance be-

[91] *Official Records*, ser. I, vol. IX, 705–706, vol. XXXIV, 945. More lengthy treatments of Unionist sentiment in north Texas are: Sam Acheson and Julie Ann Hudson O'Connell (eds.), "George Washington Diamond's Account of the Great Hanging at Gainesville, 1862," *Southwestern Historical Quarterly*, LXVI, 331–414; Claude Elliott, "Union Sentiment in Texas, 1861–1865," *ibid.*, L, 453–56; Floyd F. Ewing, Jr., "Origins of Unionist Sentiment on the West Texas Frontier," *West Texas Historical Association Year Book*, XXXII, 21–29; Ewing, "Unionist Sentiment on the Northwest Texas Frontier," *ibid.*, XXXIII, 58–70.

cause vengeful enrolling officers soon used it to punish or otherwise intimidate them.

Was there no justice? the Unionists cried. Already they had known much suffering because of what they believed. At least a third of the population in that area consisted of Germans and other immigrants who had not been assimilated into the Southern culture and who had a passionate distaste for its institutions, especially slavery. When they refused to support secession or to volunteer in the army, soldiers and loyal Southern citizens heckled and otherwise antagonized them. In July, 1862, this intimidation became so severe that Unionists met on Bear Creek and organized companies to protect themselves. General Hamilton P. Bee, commanding the western subdistrict, promptly declared the counties of Gillespie, Kerr, Kendall, Medina, Comal, and Bexar in a state of open rebellion against the Confederacy and sent Captain James Duff, with a company, to restore order. A vicious, violent man even in the eyes of his own troops, Duff hanged or shot or whiplashed any German who spoke out against the cause; on August 10, 1862, a cavalry detachment under his orders massacred some thirty-four Unionists, on their way to Mexico, on a little-known bend of the Nueces River near the trail connecting Fort Clark and Fort Concho.[92] After that no German dared to speak out.

Was there no justice? they wondered in silence. For when "Prince John" Magruder from Virginia took command, Unionists knew even more suffering than before. That winter enrolling officers, under orders from Magruder himself to enforce the letter of the conscript laws, came into German towns and tacked up draft notices to the beat of drums. Soon

[92] Robert W. Shook, "The Battle of the Nueces, August 10, 1862," *Southwestern Historical Quarterly*, LXVI, 31–42; John W. Sansom, *Battle of the Nueces in Kinney County, Texas, Aug. 10, 1862*, 1–15; R. H. Williams, *With the Border Ruffians: Memoirs of the Far West, 1852–1868*, 222; Gilbert C. Benjamin, *The Germans in Texas*, 90–95; Don H. Biggers, *German Pioneers in Texas*, 57–58.

the soldiers came again and took German youth away by gunpoint and into the army by law. German fathers protested. They sent to the governor a petition denouncing the draft as a "despotic decree" and asking the Texas government to protect their "indisputable rights" as "free citizens" and refuse to comply with the draft laws.[93] The government, though, could do nothing, and enrolling captains continued to draft Unionists with open satisfaction. Finally, in the spring of 1863, the Unionists had taken enough. They armed themselves with flintlock muskets and threatened to fight any Confederates who tried to force them into jail or into the army.[94] In North Texas, in the areas around San Antonio, Gillespie, and Austin, and all along the Río Grande, angry Unionists were on the verge of a general uprising against Confederate despotism.[95]

Over in Austin, Commander Ford reviewed reports of clashes between Unionists and Confederates with growing apprehension. He feared that, if allowed to continue, they might soon develop into a reign of terror in which hundreds of men and women and children might lose their lives. Accordingly, in the summer of 1863, Ford pleaded with General Magruder to put a stop to the drafting of Unionist men. "The man of one party," Ford reasoned, "could not honestly serve in the ranks of the other." Moreover, should Confederates continue to force "men into our ranks who believed we were wrong," they would "desert us at a critical period and carry news to their friends—our enemies—calculated to cause our defeat." To avoid this and to avoid further bloodshed, Ford urged Magruder as well as Confederates all over the state to adopt a "policy of kindly treatment" toward

[93] *Texas Almanac–Extra* (Austin), December 28, 1862; North, *Five Years in Texas,* 159–60, 168, 170–71.

[94] Elliott, "Union Sentiment in Texas, 1861–1865" *Southwestern Historical Quarterly,* L, 456–75; Fremantle, *The Fremantle Diary,* 43.

[95] Elliott, "Union Sentiment in Texas, 1861–1865" *Southwestern Historical Quarterly,* L, 472–75.

the Unionists in an effort to secure "neutrality in action and to a degree in feeling."[96]

Apparently, Ford was most convincing in his appeal. At the time he made it, General Magruder was preoccupied with a dangerous series of Federal assaults on the Texas coast and was hardly in a mood to be lenient with Unionist sympathizers. Yet he gave Ford a hearing and ultimately agreed to what the colonel asked. Ford then ordered his enrolling captains to leave Unionists alone. As a result the clashes between them began to subside.[97]

But not before some 2,132 Unionists, knowing that they might end up in a hangman's noose for what they believed, left their homes to join the Federal Army. At least 1,500 of them enlisted in Union forces beyond the Texas border. The others remained in the state to form their own Federal commands—the 1st and 2nd Texas Cavalry regiments—which in 1864 would fight against Rip Ford, the man who had done so much to get them clemency.[98]

All of this—the inequity and violence that resulted from a rigorous use (or misuse) of the draft—suggests that General Magruder was weak as a district commander who had to deal with civilians as well as to lead soldiers, who had to respect civilian rights and civilian authority, and who had to treat gently those Texans having a genuine antipathy to the Confederacy and its cause. Magruder apparently cared little for any of these. He was a field rather than a desk commander, a fighter rather than an administrator; consequently, he either ignored administrative matters, leaving them to his subdistrict commanders who in some cases were incompetent, or he dealt with such matters superficially, in a

[96] Ford, *Rip Ford's Texas*, 333.

[97] *Ibid.*, 335–36; Magruder to W. R. Boggs, May 29, 1863, *Official Records*, ser. I, vol. XXVI, pt. 2, p. 22.

[98] See Frank H. Smyrl, "Texans in the Union Army, 1861–1865," *Southwestern Historical Quarterly*, LXV, 234–50; and Elliott, "Union Sentiment in Texas, 1861–1865," *ibid.*, L, 448–77.

hurry, so that he could give most of his attention to battle and to regaining the glory he had lost in the earlier part of the Civil War.

For Magruder came to Texas determined to wipe out a black mark on his otherwise impressive military record. He had received it during the Seven Days campaign back in Virginia (June 25–July 1, 1862) when superior officers charged him with inefficiency in command (he had failed to press McClellan's retiring forces vigorously, had not exploited a serious gap in the Federal lines, asking for reinforcements instead of attacking, had been repulsed with heavy losses at Savage Station, and had taken a wrong road at Malvern Hill). Magruder, believing that he had been mistreated in official reports, opened correspondence with Robert E. Lee, and argued with intensity—if not with literal accuracy—in his own behalf. Lee was most disappointed in Magruder, for the commanding general wanted officers whom he could work with as well as who would fight.[99] The upshot was that Magruder was transferred to far-away Texas. A sensitive man beneath his tough exterior, he left Virginia with a promise to restore his reputation through bold and brilliant combat leadership.

Thus when he assumed command on November 29, 1862, he reviewed the military situation and made battle plans with a single-minded purpose that caused him to ignore his administrative duties. The first thing he had to do was re-capture the vital seaport of Galveston. It had fallen back in October when eight Federal warships steamed into the harbor and demanded immediate surrender. Confederate defenses under the over-all command of Colonel J. J. Cook answered with an artillery salvo, but then gave up after eleven-inch Federal guns disabled Fort Point and fired a few blasts at the city itself.

[99] *Official Records*, ser. I, vol. IX, pt. 2, pp. 494, 687; *Dictionary of American Biography*, XII, 205.

The Confederates were still evacuating Galveston when Magruder started making plans to retake it. Before he could consolidate his scattered forces, though, the enemy boats landed troops of occupation on December 25. They would not stay there long, Magruder promised. He would drive them back into the sea and soon. During the next five days he gathered a motley assortment of horse and infantry—the 26th Texas Cavalry under Colonel S. B. Debray, a sophisticated Frenchman who had been schooled at the famous St. Cyr Military Academy; several other cavalry groups, detachments, and companies under Colonel Tom Green of New Mexico fame; and some volunteer infantry. Magruder also had a battery of artillery and two battered river steamers that had been converted into warships—the *Bayou City* and the *Neptune*. The plan of attack called for the land forces to move into the city under cover of darkness while the gunboats descending from the mouth of the Trinity River attacked and sank the Federal war vessels anchored in the harbor. Aboard the Confederate ships were a number of dismounted cavalry—"horse marines"—who would fire at the enemy from behind cotton bales stacked on deck.[100]

A daring plan this was, yet one that might well succeed if the gunboats could disable the enemy vessels and gain control of the harbor. At 1:00 A.M. on New Year's morning, 1863, while the Federals slept after a night of heavy drinking, Magruder led his land forces quietly into the city; after the moon had set, they swept the wharves with howitzers,

[100] For reports of the fighting at Galveston in October, 1862, see *Official Records*, ser. I, vol. XV, 151–53, 148–49, and *Official Records of the Union and Confederate Navies in the War of Rebellion*, ser. I, vol. XIX, 254–60. My account of the Confederate recapture of Galveston, unless otherwise cited, was drawn from the following articles and sources: Alwyn Barr, "Texas Coastal Defense, 1861–1865," *Southwestern Historical Quarterly*, XLV, 14–18; Charles C. Cumberland, "The Confederate Loss and Recapture of Galveston, 1862–1863," *ibid.*, LI, 109–30; Magruder's report, February 26, 1863, *Official Records*, ser. I, vol. XV, 211–20; and Robert M. Franklin, *Battle of Galveston, January 1st, 1863.*

then stormed Federal camps there with pistols blazing. The Federals somehow rallied and drove them off, but the Texans crying their famous yell charged again and again. The fighting, begun as a surprise attack, soon developed into a respectable battle as the warships out on the water lowered their cannon and raked the streets where the Texans were alternately advancing and retiring.

When the Confederate sailors above the city saw the flashes of the Union guns, they steered their boats out into the choppy bay waters and began their rush toward the heavily armed *Harriet Lane*. As they approached in the dim morning haze, Tom Green's horse marines picked off Union sailors running along the *Lane*'s decks; Green himself shot a courageous young officer trying to discharge a loaded cannon single-handed. Suddenly the *Neptune* took a direct hit from the *Lane*'s pivot gun, lurched dangerously, then veered off into shallow water where it sank. The *Bayou City* continued its advance, though, with Green's sharpshooters still peppering the *Lane*'s deck. Their fire was so blistering that Union sailors to save their lives had to take cover below. At last the Texan vessel bumped into the *Lane*'s starboard side, and the horse marines stormed aboard, captured what remained of the crew, and struck the colors.

The Texans found the *Lane's* deck strewn with dead and wounded and with pieces of exploded shell. An elderly Texan major who came aboard to help the wounded saw "his own son"—a Federal lieutenant—"lying on the deck mortally wounded." The major did not cry or say anything as he took his son in his arms and gently rocked him back and forth as the boy died. The sight of them moved both Confederates and Unionists to tears, for here was a living example of how this tragic war had torn families apart as it had the Union, setting brother against brother and—here on the deck of the *Lane*—a father against a son. When the son

129

was dead, the father permitted himself a brief cry, hugged the boy to him, then laid him back and went on to help the other wounded as the battle of Galveston moved into its final stage.[101]

The other Texans on board the *Lane* crowded along the rail to listen to the racket of cannon and musketry coming from the town and to see what the remaining Federal warships would do. The men let out a resounding cheer when they saw, quite suddenly, white flags go up over the other vessels. There was an exchange of shouts; the Texans demanded surrender, the Federals refused. But they had had enough and by mass consent agreed to withdraw. As they steered their boats out of the harbor, they passed the Union flagship, which had run aground earlier in the fighting; suddenly a terrific explosion blew the ship apart—a premature detonation which killed the Union fleet commander and several others. For the navy this was the final blow in a humiliating New Year's battle in which almost everything had gone wrong.

Yet it was even worse for the Federal infantry, still fighting on the wharves, who looked on in horror as the Federal fleet steamed around the burning flagship and headed toward the open sea. Without naval support, the infantry soon fell to Magruder's charging Texans.

And so, a Confederate general who had come to Texas determined to prove himself had won an astonishing victory which dealt Union naval prestige a severe blow. His men praised him as a general who fought at the front of battle instead of the rear.[102] Civilians, too, all over the state, lauded him, and the legislature in a joint resolution commended

---

[101] "Texas and Texans in the Civil War, 1861–1865," in *Comprehensive History of Texas*, II, 533.

[102] *Ibid.*, 531; Ford, *Rip Ford's Texas*, 343.

him for heroism and then gave him a standing ovation.[103] In the months that followed, political leaders would of course come to regard Magruder as a tyrant in his administrative capacities; yet, even then, they would concede grudgingly that as a field commander this Virginian was indubitably bold and effective.

Magruder himself had little time to enjoy all the praise. The Federal gunboats came back in a few days to blockade Galveston and to bombard Confederate installations all along the coast. The general feared that this might be the advance of an all-out invasion which Texans had been expecting since the opening of the war. He reinforced his batteries with a few guns from the interior and warned his field officers to expect the worst.[104]

The long-awaited invasion came that fall. On September 8, 1863, a Federal force of four gunboats and twenty-two troop transports carrying some 4,000 men steamed into Sabine Pass, about sixty miles up the coast from Galveston. Confederate forces at the Pass, reinforced months earlier on orders from Magruder himself, consisted of forty-seven men with six cannon and two cottonclad rams under the command of Lieutenant Richard W. Dowling. Despite the odds, the Texan artillerymen, firing at an incredible clip of one shell every two minutes, disabled two enemy gunboats, took 350 prisoners, and turned back the invasion.[105]

Repelled at Sabine Pass, the Federals decided to invade

103 Texas Senate Journal, 9th Leg., 1st called sess., February 2–March 7, 1863; Lubbock, Six Decades in Texas, 451–53.

104 Barr, "Texas Coastal Defense, 1861–1865," Southwestern Historical Quarterly, LXV, 18–19, 21–23.

105 Confederate reports of the battle of Sabine Pass are in Official Records, ser. I, vol. XXVI, pt. 1, pp. 309–12; reports of Union naval officers are in Official Records, Navies, ser. I, vol. XX, 517–61. See also the following articles: Andrew Forest Muir, "Dick Dowling and the Battle of Sabine Pass," Civil War History, IV, 407–428; and Alwyn Barr, "Sabine Pass, September, 1863," Texas Military History, II, 17–22.

Texas through the lower Río Grande Valley. On November 1, 1863, some 4,500 troops under Nathaniel P. Banks landed at the mouth of the Great River and overran Brownsville, cutting off the all-important Confederate trade route through Matamoros. The invading force then split into two columns: one drove up the river to occupy Río Grande City; the other swept up the coast to capture Corpus Christi, Aransas Pass, and all of the Matagorda Peninsula.[106]

As the Federals continued to advance against mild resistance, Magruder took the field himself, leaving his immediate staff to tend administrative functions. The general gathered a small force including walking wounded and went after the Federals around Matagorda Bay, but he was so badly outnumbered and outgunned that he had to retreat west of the Colorado River, wrecking long stretches of the San Antonio–Gulf Coast Railroad as he went.[107]

Then, inexplicably, the Federals also retreated—back down to Matagorda Island. Unknown to Magruder, who was frantically collecting an army of home guard troops, old men, and anyone else who would fight, Federal commanders had decided to hold what they had along the coast and along the Río Grande and concentrate most of their manpower on the Red River campaign, which would take Union forces up Louisiana and into Texas from the northeast.[108]

Magruder, though, knew nothing of this. As far as he was concerned, the Federal withdrawal could mean any number of things. It could mean, for instance, that they had pulled back merely to regroup and would soon advance directly into the interior toward San Antonio and Austin. Aggressive

[106] Banks to H. H. Bell, November 3, 1863; Banks to F. J. Herron, December 25, 1863, *Official Records*, ser. I, vol. XXVI, pt. 1, pp. 785, 880–81.

[107] Magruder to Boggs, December 22, 1863; Magruder to Kirby Smith, December 24, 1863, *ibid.*, pt. 2, pp. 524, 530; Houston *Tri-Weekly Telegraph*, December 2, 4, 9, 11, 1863.

[108] Special Orders No. 322, December 24, 1863; Banks to Edwin M. Stanton, April 6, 1864, *Official Records*, ser. I, vol. XXVI, pt. 1, pp. 194–95.

soldier that he was, Magruder decided to counterattack and recapture as much of the valley as possible. On December 22, 1863, he named his conscript commander, Rip Ford, to command the operation with orders to raise 2,000 men for three months' duty in the "Cavalry of the West."[109] Because Ford had a notable record as a Texas Ranger and cavalry colonel, Magruder no doubt expected much from him. Yet the colonel had considerable difficulty in getting money and men and supplies for the expedition. He was not ready to move until mid-March, 1864, and even then most of his 1,300 troops were under eighteen and over forty and were all poorly armed.[110]

On the march, new problems arose to impede Ford's progress: severe shortages of food and ammunition; attacks by Federal cavalry detachments and Mexican bandits operating along the Nueces River; and the lack of water caused by a severe drought during the past two years.[111]

While Ford moved slowly toward the Río Grande, Magruder over on the coast continued to strengthen his defenses in anticipation of a new Federal offensive. Then he received ominous news from Louisiana that Banks with 27,000 men and a powerful flotilla had launched a drive up the Red River toward Shreveport, that Texas for the first time in the war was in danger of being overrun by a truly large Federal army. Learning this, Magruder lost all interest in the Federal forces occupying the valley. On orders from Kirby Smith, he started what troops he had toward Louisiana only to collide head-on with angry civilian leaders who refused to let their soldiers leave with the enemy still

[109] Edmund P. Turner to Ford, December 22, 1863; Magruder to E. Kirby Smith, December 24, 1863, *ibid.*, vol. XXVI, pt. 2, pp. 525–26, 528–30.

[110] Ford to Turner, February 5 and 7, March 25, 1864, *ibid.*, vol. XXXIV, pt. 2, pp. 946–47, 948–49, 1083–84; Ford to Magruder, February 21, 1864, in John S. Ford, Letter Books (typescript, Archives, Texas State Library), I, 12.

[111] Ford, *Rip Ford's Texas*, 344–49.

on Texas soil.[112] In the midst of this civil-military conflict, Magruder again received news from Louisiana: Richard Taylor's army including several Texas cavalry and infantry brigades had stopped the Federals at Mansfield (April 8) and Pleasant Hill (April 9) and thrown them back down the Red River. At about the same time, in Arkansas, three Confederate cavalry divisions had overtaken and turned back a second Federal column from Little Rock.

The Federal threat in Louisiana gone, Magruder stopped feuding with civil officials and concentrated on regaining possession of the valley. He sent Colonel Ford, then at Río Grande City, a few fresh troops and cannon and urged him to attack Brownsville. Ford was rather reluctant to do so, having heard that the enemy there outnumbered him two to one, but at last he moved forward.

Through the next few weeks, Ford with some of his old fighting spirit defeated Federal cavalry detachments and their Mexican guerrilla allies in several running engagements; then, on July 30, 1864, he captured Brownsville after a week of heavy skirmishing. By mid-August, Ford's Texans had forced the enemy to abandon all of the Río Grande except Brazos Island. Once again the life-giving supply trains from Matamoros rumbled across the border heading for Confederate armies in Arkansas, Louisiana, and beyond.[113]

As the commander of Texas who had conceived the valley campaign, General Magruder took most of the credit for Ford's achievement. This brought him to the attention of E. Kirby Smith, commanding the Trans-Mississippi Department, who was looking for a good combat officer to head the

[112] See Governor Pendleton Murrah's Message to the 10th Leg., extra sess., May 11, 1865, in Pendleton Murrah, Letter Books (MS, Archives, Texas State Library), II, Bk. No. 44, pp. 73–96; Murrah to Magruder, April 7, 1864, *Official Records*, ser. I, vol. XXXIV, pt. 2, pp. 747–50; Joseph H. Parks, *General Edmund Kirby Smith, C.S.A.*, 367–68.

[113] Ford, *Rip Ford's Texas*, 353–63; Oates, "John S. 'Rip' Ford, Prudent Cavalryman, C. S. A.," *Southwestern Historical Quarterly*, LXIV, 304–305.

Arkansas District, where Confederates were planning a new offensive against the Union forces that held the northern half of the state. Though Magruder had a bad reputation as an impulsive administrator with "an utter disregard for the law," Kirby Smith nevertheless thought he had energy and ability and on August 4, 1865, transferred him to Arkansas.[114]

The Texans viewed Magruder's transfer with mixed emotions. An administrative tyrant was gone, but so was a dependable warrior who had perhaps done more than anyone else to save their homes from the Federal invaders. Would the new district commander, a reticent general named J. G. Walker, prove as effective once the Federals renewed their offensive against Texas? And another invasion would indubitably come, the Texans believed, since the enemy had retained a strong garrison on Brazos Island.[115]

The fear of invasion continued to haunt Texans throughout the final year of the war. Every Confederate defeat beyond their borders—Price's cavalry disaster in Missouri that winter, the fall of Georgia and the Carolinas to Sherman's advancing army—portended a new Federal offensive against Texas. By February, 1865, the invasion jitters had developed into a kind of state-wide paranoia. In the valley, Rip Ford's cavalry kept a constant watch on Brazos Island, lest a Federal striking force land there. All along the coast, from Corpus Christi to Sabine Pass, Texan sentinels scanned the moving Gulf waters for a sign of enemy ships. Over in Houston, at district headquarters, Walker and his staff studied reports of Confederate losses on every front with the distressed expressions of men who might soon have to face a prison stockade. Then, on the night of March 6, a Con-

114 *Official Records*, ser. I, vol. XXXIV, pt. 2, pp. 868–70, vol. XLI, pt. 2, p. 1039.
115 *Ibid.*; Blessington, *Walker's Texas Division*, 73–74; Roberts, "Texas," in *Confederate Military History*, XI, 125–28.

federate secret service agent fresh from New Orleans came to headquarters with alarming intelligence. At New Orleans a Federal invasionary army of 40,000 men, maybe more, was preparing to strike the Texas coast sometime in the next few weeks. His story was hardly substantiated, but Walker and his officers were in such a nervous state that they believed it without question. The next morning, March 7, Walker sent a frantic message to Kirby Smith at Shreveport: a huge invasionary force was coming across the Gulf toward Texas; Walker had to have reinforcements in a hurry.[116] Apparently, Kirby Smith also had the invasion jitters. He took Walker at his word and moved swiftly to meet the impending danger: he ordered Joseph Shelby's cavalry to Shreveport, Thomas J. Churchill's infantry to Marshall, John H. Forney's infantry to Huntsville, and General Magruder back to Houston to replace Walker as district commander. If an invasion were coming, then a fighting commander must be in Texas to meet it.[117]

Through the weeks the Confederates waited, but they saw not a sign of invasion, not a single sign. April came and passed. Then on May 11, in the valley, one of Rip Ford's cavalry patrols spotted enemy troops coming off Brazos Island in a blinding rainstorm. Was this the invasion? Had a Union army landed on the island undetected? At Brownsville, Ford and General James E. Slaughter, who the previous fall had taken command of the Río Grande subdistrict, called on Magruder for reinforcements and fast. On May 13, while Slaughter waited for help to arrive, Ford with nearly a thousand cavalry rode southeast to Palmito Ranch, where the Texan patrol had already engaged the invaders. In an explosion of daring, Ford ordered an attack. His

<hr>

[116] *Official Records*, ser. I, vol. XLVII, pt. 1, p. 1412.

[117] Boggs to Magruder, March 8, 1865, *ibid.*, 1416; Kirby Smith to Walker March 22, 1865, *ibid.*, 1442.

Texans charged fiercely and drove the Federals back to Brazos Island in a wild, running fight.

As it turned out, however, the Texans had not stopped an invasion, but had merely whipped the regular island garrison composed mainly of Negro troops. From a prisoner, the Texans learned that General Lee had surrendered at Appomattox over a month earlier and that the Federals on the island, having heard the news, had started for Brownsville expecting the Texans to capitulate as well. The engagement at Palmito, the prisoner concluded, had been an awful mistake—a mistake that, as it happened, was the last land battle fought in the Confederacy.[118]

The reports of Confederate collapse east of the river started a nervous, frightened ripple over the state. General Magruder called on his troops to stand by the colors in spite of what had happened in Virginia.[119] Governor Murrah also pleaded for loyalty in these dark moments. "Look at the bloody and desolate tracks of the invader through Georgia and South Carolina," Murrah warned, "and see the fate that awaits you. . . . Rally around the battle scarred and well known flag of the Confederacy and uphold your state government in its purity and integrity—There is no other hope for safety for you and yours."[120]

In response, civilians and soldiers gathered in mass demonstrations to pledge their allegiance and their lives to the Confederacy. "If our people," cried a soldier in a meeting

118 Federal reports of the battle at Palmito Ranch are in *ibid.*, 265–68. For the Confederate side see Ford, *Rip Ford's Texas*, 388–92; Ford's article in the San Antonio *Express*, October 10, 1890; Ford's account of the battle in Roberts, "Texas," in *Confederate Military History*, XI, 126–29; and Captain W. H. D. Carrington's account in Brown, *History of Texas from 1685 to 1892*, II, 431–36.

119 *Texas State Gazette* (Austin), May 3, 1865; Galveston *Tri-Weekly News*, April 23, May 12, 1865; Parks, *General Edmund Kirby Smith, C.S.A.*, 457–58.

120 Murrah's Proclamation, April 27, 1865, in Murrah, Letter Books, III, Bk. No. 45, p. 12.

at Millican, Texas, "and our TROOPS would come to the rescue as they should do; if they would unite as one man; the Trans-Mississippi could defy the combined powers of Yankeedom."[121]

Then came the crushing news that the Army of Tennessee —General Hood's old command—had given up at Greensboro, North Carolina, and that Confederate forces in Arkansas and parts of Louisiana had disintegrated.

This seemed to take everything out of Texas troops. Their patriotism and tenacity gave way to fear—a fear of coming violence, of some cataclysmic doom. On May 15 troops at the Galveston garrison mutinied and took off for their homes in fear and panic; at the same time men at other garrisons all along the coast demonstrated an open disregard for discipline and organization.[122] Magruder set out for Houston in a desperate effort to keep his military units together. But as he rode he was confronted every hour with the evidence that his district was crumbling to pieces around him. Fully half the troops in the western subdistrict had deserted. The remaining half refused to bring them back, thinking it "useless for the Trans-Mississippi Department to undertake what the Cis-Mississippi Department has failed to do." Magruder returned to Houston a bitter, defeated man. He wired Kirby Smith at Shreveport that all was lost, that to prevent further rioting the commander must let all the troops go home by regiments "with as little damage to the community as possible." "For God's sake," Magruder cried, "act or let me act."[123]

Kirby Smith, though, wired him to hold on at all costs: the commander had decided to move his headquarters from

121 Heartsill, *Fourteen Hundred and Ninety-One Days*, 239–42; Sarah Kate (Stone) Holmes, *Brokenburn: The Journal of Kate Stone, 1861–1868* (ed. John Q. Anderson), 333, 340–43, 344–45.

122 Galveston *Tri-Weekly News*, May 15, 17, 1865.

123 Magruder to E. Kirby Smith, May 16, 1865, *Official Records*, ser. I, vol. XLVIII, pt. 2, p. 1308.

Shreveport to Houston where he would "fight to the bitter end."

But the end had already come. When Kirby Smith reached Huntsville, he found mobs of "disorderly soldiery thronging the roads"—the remnants of Forney's infantry division.[124] Things were even worse at Hempstead where cavalry outfits had disbanded so that the men could go home to protect their families from "roving bands of thieves and robbers."[125] All across east and south Texas, these gangs—many of them including draft dodgers and deserters and Unionists—pillaged towns and bushwhacked Confederate soldiers.

At last Kirby Smith reached Houston, but by that time everything in Texas had crumbled—all the cavalry and infantry had disbanded and control over troops and jayhawkers and everyone else was gone. On May 22, Kirby Smith and Magruder were generals without an army.[126] Several days later they heard that on May 26, Kirby Smith's chief of staff had surrendered the Trans-Mississippi Department at New Orleans and that a Union steamer was bringing the surrender terms to Galveston for Kirby Smith's signature. There was little he could do but give it, and on June 2, with Magruder at his side, he boarded the ship in the harbor and signed away the last, lingering hope of the South.[127]

Soon after, fearing that the Yankees might persecute them, the two men joined a column of die-hard Southerners on their way to Mexico. In the ranks were cavalrymen from Missouri, including such commanders as Joseph Shelby and Sterling Price. Governor Murrah of Texas, too, was there. So were two other Confederate governors and several lesser politicians and private citizens. They moved

---

[124] Parks, *General Edmund Kirby Smith, C.S.A.,* 473–74.

[125] Heartsill, *Fourteen Hundred and Ninety-One Days,* 244.

[126] Parks, *General Edmund Kirby Smith, C.S.A.,* 473.

[127] *Official Records,* ser. I, vol. XLVIII, pt. 2, pp. 600–601; ser. II, vol. VIII, 717.

on through Eagle Pass, stopped at the Río Grande so that the troopers could bury their flags in the muddy waters, and then rode out of a land whose people had fought hard and pitifully for a cause that was perhaps lost from the beginning.[128] For those tired, empty men who headed across the Mexican plain toward Monterrey, as well as for thousands of Southerners who remained in Texas, in Arkansas, Georgia, and everywhere else in the South, the "bright dream" of the Confederacy was over. Perhaps they could all —as a young soldier on his way home to Marshall expressed it—perhaps they could all "fall down in the dust and weep over our great misfortune, our great calamities."[129]

128 John N. Edwards, *Shelby and His Men; Or, The War in the West*, 543–51.
129 Heartsill, *Fourteen Hundred and Ninety-One Days*, 245.

PART TWO

*With this introduction we may pass from
the legendary duel of Syriac saga to consider
a few of the examples offered by history.*

—Arnold J. Toynbee

The Civil War ended for all time Texan visions of conquest and empire, either as an independent republic or as an affiliate of a loose confederation of Southern states. Now that their dreams of independence from the United States and of a new national destiny had been destroyed on the battlefield, Texans had no choice but to remain in the Union as citizens of a government which they and most of their descendants would always regard with a certain provincial suspicion, and to make the most of their own land and the resources it contained.

As Texans set about utilizing those resources in the post-war era, the martial spirit that had dominated their lives in the antebellum period gradually gave way to a highly competitive economic spirit. From the 1870's on, Texans proved time and again that their best talents lay not in military adventure but in bold and imaginative economic enterprise. Between 1866 and 1880, for example, Texans not only developed an impressive agricultural and merchant trade and constructed over 8,000 miles of railroads, but helped make the cattle business a major United States industry, as Texas cowmen stocked ranges on the northern Great Plains and drove nearly four and a quarter million longhorns to Kansas railroad centers where they were shipped to slaughtering houses in the East.

More important than the deeds of the cattlemen, a handful of prospectors and geologists discovered oil beneath the Texas surface and set in motion a spectacular series of oil booms that transformed formerly Confederate Texas from a cattle kingdom into a sprawling industrial empire. But the transformation did not occur without violence; indeed, some of the worst examples of hate and human debauchery on record took place in such wide-open boom towns as Beaumont, Burkburnett, Ranger, and Borger, out on the moon-like plains of the Texas Panhandle, where violence was so

143

rampant that the governor had to call out the National Guard and place Borger under martial law.

Still, if there was a recurrence of the old frontier lawlessness in Texas' oil towns, the positive results of the oil boom outweighed the violence that accompanied it, for it provided Texas with fabulous wealth, not only for economic growth but for educational and humanitarian activities as well. And the final reckoning still cannot be made, because the state's multibillion-dollar oil and petrochemical industry, combined with the scientific and medical facilities available in the Greater Houston area, enabled Texas to invite the National Aeronautics and Space Administration to establish its headquarters there. NASA's move to Houston in 1961 precipitated still another boom, one that opened unprecedented new dimensions for growth in industry, urban planning, medicine, and education. And the space boom has only just begun.

The two accounts that follow, departing from the martial themes of Part One, focus on the most significant of the oil bonanzas—those at Spindletop in 1901 and 1925—and on NASA's operations in Houston in the early 1960's. Both narratives attempt to re-create the human experience of those two episodes and to suggest the new technical and psychological frontiers which they opened for Texas and for the nation at large.

VI

Roaring
Spindletop

THE Civil War had scarcely ended when a few former Confederates, looking for a fast way to recoup their fortunes, began prospecting for oil in East Texas. While oil during the Reconstruction period was not quite the new El Dorado it would later become, there had been considerable oil stock promotion during the war itself, and prospectors were convinced that oil now had excellent commercial possibilities.

One of those prospectors was a former Confederate from Melrose named Lynis T. Barrett. Before the war had interrupted his work, Barrett had actually started drilling a well at an oil spring on the Skillern property near Melrose, a static little East Texas community about ten miles east of Nacogdoches. Now that hostilities had ended, Barrett returned to Melrose with plans to resume his drilling operations. If he could bring in a producer such as Edwin L. Drake had drilled in Pennsylvania in 1859 (the nation's first oil well), Barrett believed he could make a profitable business for himself and perhaps start an economic boom for all Nacogdoches County.

On October 9, 1865, only four months after Kirby Smith

had officially surrendered the Trans-Mississippi Department to Union forces, Barrett formed one of Texas' first oil companies with three business associates and after some delay set about drilling on the Skillern tract a second time. Using a crude drill powered by a steam engine, Barrett and his colleagues bore down to about one hundred feet, where "the auger suddenly dropped about 6 inches." In a moment, "pure oil several inches deep came to the surface."[1] Former Confederate Barrett had brought in Texas' first producer, a harbinger of good fortune that caused considerable excitement among the citizens of Melrose. They came out to stare at the oil well and to speculate about the black underground lake which Barrett insisted lay beneath their feet. In the meantime, Barrett himself traveled to Pennsylvania and persuaded a company there "to come to our field in Texas with about $5,000 worth of machinery suitable to the development of oil." But just when oil fever was high in Nacogdoches County, the Pennsylvania company backed out. Congressional Reconstruction had just begun, the company pointed out, and "the unsettled condition of the country," together with the low price of oil, made it "inadvisable to prosecute the work further."[2]

Barrett, immeasurably disappointed, tried to get financial help from others. But nobody was willing to gamble a dime on Barrett's project in these uncertain times, and eventually he had to abandon his well in despair.

But if Barrett had failed to develop Oil Springs into a competitive oil field, he had nevertheless made East Texas quite oil conscious. After the vicissitudes of Reconstruction were over, another group of East Texas oil men started drilling near Barrett's abandoned well. In 1887 they brought in a producer that was impressive for Texas, as nearly three

[1] Quoted in Carl Coke Rister, *Oil! Titan of the Southwest*, 5. See also C. A. Warner, *Texas Oil and Gas Since 1543*, 6.
[2] Rister, *Oil!*, 6.

hundred barrels of oil flowed out over the ground. Soon other oil promoters and drillers arrived at the field, and by 1890 some ninety wells had been drilled and a rudimentary refinery constructed there. Barrett's dream had come true in more ways than one, for both Melrose and Nacogdoches were profiting from the influx of men and money; everywhere, on street corners and in saloons and cafes, oil monopolized conversations. As a former Confederate had already written an old comrade-in-arms, oil had become the "great excitement of this age. . . . It promises to lay in the shade the great 'South Sea Bubble' or any other bubble of any age. This region of Texas will be wild upon the subject in a few months . . . and if we are prepared for the excitement, we will make our fortune. What is the use of toiling and struggling with aching brains and weary hands for bread, when gold so temptingly invites you to reach out and clutch it?"[3]

These were prophetic words indeed, for in 1894 another field was discovered some 130 miles to the northwest, at Corsicana, where derricks "sprang up as if by magic" until a veritable oil well jungle obscured the sky along the east side of town. But the opening of the Nacogdoches and Corsicana fields, neither of them large enough to compete with fields in Pennsylvania, was only a prelude to perhaps the most spectacular oil strike of them all, that which took place near a quiet little trading center in southeast Texas, some twenty miles inland from the Gulf Coast. Texas and the nation's petroleum industry were never to be the same.

Except for an incongruous, fifty-foot drilling rig on Big Hill just below town, Beaumont was hardly distinguishable from any other rice and sawmill community in the American

3 *Ibid.*, 4.

South of the 1890's. The inhabitants were nearly all native Texans, spoke in a rich East Texas drawl, and fitted the stereotype of the provincial small-town Southerner. They took pride in their Confederate heritage and professed to follow, even as the nineteenth century drew to a close, the old virtues of Jefferson's agrarian republic: simplicity, honest toil, and punctiliousness. They were habitual churchgoers, although they saw nothing contradictory, let alone un-Christian, in their segregation of the Negro or in a little "cussin'" and "drinkin'" now and then to let off steam. They were unabashed conformists, too, and would stare at anyone who did something bizarre—something that did not promise immediate material rewards (like drilling an oil well, for instance)—as though he were a green zoo bird.

That is why Beaumont citizens had been watching Patillo Higgins' activities on Big Hill, a sandy dome four miles south of town, on a swamp plains near the Neches River, with such a mixture of cynicism and curiosity. Higgins, a one-armed, self-educated jack-of-all-trades, the son of a local blacksmith, had been drilling for oil there almost six years to a day—since late February, 1893. But all he had found so far was a seemingly unfathomable layer of quicksand; three times his drills had failed to penetrate it. And now the Gladys City Oil, Gas and Manufacturing Company, which Higgins had formed with borrowed money and which he had named after a little girl in his Baptist Sunday School class, was nearly bankrupt. Beaumont merchants, discussing Higgins' oil rig over coffee in the local cafes, shook their heads. Why didn't Patillo give up this harebrained scheme before he lost every dollar he had? Everybody knew there was no oil under Big Hill. Unless—as some said—Patillo was slightly touched in the head. The old-timers, who leaned against store fronts and spat tobacco juice in the shaded street, ribbed the prospector goodnaturedly—"the Millionaire," they called him—when he came hurrying into town with some other money-raising proposition burning in his head. But their humor turned to pity, too, when Beaumont's bankers refused to help him. No sir, they told Higgins, nobody in his right mind would risk any more money on this wild and foolish dream. Why, any amateur geologist could tell you there was no oil around here. Why didn't he put his faith and his money into something profitable, such as a rice mill or a furniture factory?[4]

But Higgins refused to quit. He was convinced that the sulfurous gas seeping from Big Hill was an incontestible sign that beneath it, perhaps beneath the very ground he was now walking over, lay the greatest pool of oil in the world. But could he convince anybody else? In desperation, he ran an advertisement in an eastern trade journal. In June, 1899, a former Austrian sailor named Captain Anthony Lucas turned up in Beaumont, said he had seen the ad, and inquired about Higgins' project. Lucas was a broad-shouldered, slim-waisted man, with a full moustache and an engaging accent; he was also an expert mining engineer with an itch to drill for oil—and the money to finance it, too. After inspecting the hill and reviewing Higgins' drilling record, Lucas signed a lease and option-sale contract. On June 20 he started drilling.

But the captain fared no better than Higgins. When he too ran low on money, he tried to borrow from local promoters as Higgins had done, but nobody in Jefferson County—or in nearby Houston—was willing to help. Lucas even tried to get assistance from Standard Oil Company, which had a monopoly on the nation's oil market, but a representa-

[4] E. DeGolyer, "Anthony F. Lucas at Spindletop," *Southwest Review*, XXXI (Fall, 1945), 84–85; Ruth Sheldon Knowles, *The Greatest Gamblers: The Epic of American Oil Exploration*, 23; and James A. Clark and Michel T. Halbouty, *Spindletop*, 3–27. I have also examined material pertaining to Spindletop in the DeGolyer Collection, Southern Methodist University Library, Dallas, Texas.

tive of the company took one look at Big Hill and shook his head. "You have completely misled yourself," he told Lucas, "and I know it has been expensive. You will never find oil here."

"I'm sorry you can't see the possibilities, Mr. Payne," was all the captain said.[5] After Payne had gone back east, Lucas invested what remained of his own savings in order to keep on drilling. He and his wife, who was the daughter of a wealthy Georgia physician, lived in an unplastered shack with apple boxes and egg crates for furniture. But then he ran into more trouble and finally, in March, 1900, had to give up drilling.

By now Beaumonters had ceased to pay much attention to Lucas' foolishness. If the foreigner was too stubborn to go back to salt mining as the experts advised him to do, then he did not even merit their pity. The old-timers went back to talking about the weather and the rice crop.

But not everybody had written Lucas' operations off. William Battle Phillips of the Texas Geological Survey had faith in the captain's work and suggested that he approach Guffey and Galey, a company that had done some drilling at Corsicana, Texas. Lucas did, and to his surprise the Pittsburgh company promptly assumed the captain's financial obligations for a sizable portion of his lease, and he was able to start drilling again. This time he used the new rotary method, drilling with a solid pipe that had a bit fastened to the end, which bore through the quicksand and on into the "hard foundation" underneath.

Without warning, on the brisk cloudless morning of January 10, 1901, the crew working around the oil rig heard a weird hissing noise and then saw mud spewing out of the well. They scurried for cover. There was a racking explosion which sent pieces of pipe clanging up through the derrick,

[5] Clark and Halbouty, *Spindletop*, 56.

followed by a sustained deafening roar as black oil came gushing over the top of the derrick, spraying the ground for yards around. In about fifteen minutes Captain Lucas approached the hill in a buggy, whipping his horse faster and faster when he saw the miraculous spectacle ahead. "Al! Al! What is it!" Lucas cried as he tripped head forward out of the buggy, picked himself up, and ran toward the driller. "When I told him oil," Al said later, "he exclaimed, 'Thank God.' "

But, "now that we have got her, boys," the captain shouted to his crew, "how are we going to close her up?"[6] As they labored to get a lid over the well hole, farmers rode over to see what all the commotion was about. One of them stood under the raining oil for a few moments, then mounted his horse and like "an oil-saturated Paul Revere" rode into Beaumont crying, "It's oil! On the hill! And the damn stuff has ruined my home and farm."[7] Oil was flowing out of the well at an incredible rate of between 75,000 and 100,000 barrels a day.

An earthquake could not have stirred Beaumont more. Oil? The foreigner had struck oil on Big Hill? While the farmer rode down and back up the streets crying the fabulous news, Beaumonters climbed on their roof tops and raced in buggies to the edge of town to get a look at the black geyser off on the horizon. At the same time the news clicked out over the local telegraph, and before long headlines in newspapers all over the United States were blazing: "Oil gusher at Beaumont."

The little town was quite unprepared for what followed. When five more wells, drilled by an assortment of local and out-of-state promoters, blew in that March, Beaumont was literally inundated with oil experts, oil company executives,

[6] Rister, *Oil!*, 58.
[7] Clark and Halbouty, *Spindletop*, 56.

wheeler-dealer promoters, speculators, down-and-out day laborers, and moon-eyed Texas sightseers who arrived on special trains from Houston—six of them were running daily now. Men waded with their "trousers rolled to the knees" through "raw oil" to see the spewing wells or to drill their own.[8] Thanks to the tremendous demand for oil which the new automobile industry had created, the rush to Beaumont was already quite as frenzied as the gold rush to the Far West had been. Mass exposure in the newspapers also helped, and so did the railroads. Every day now they brought a new crowd of prospectors hell-bent on making their fortunes in Beaumont's black gold. Houston, trying to capitalize on the boom too, billed itself as "The Gateway to Beaumont." And Beaumont itself adopted a royal name (as is the American custom for spectacular events): "The Queen of the Neches," where "You'll SEE a gusher gushing."

In point of fact, you could see a dozen of them gushing by then, and new ones were blowing in virtually every day. By the time winter turned to spring, there were 214 wells dotting the hill, 120 of them mashed together on one fifteen-acre tract. The oil they produced was good high-grade petroleum—so good, in fact, that the Southern Pacific Railroad announced on May 15 that henceforth its trains would use Beaumont oil in place of coal. This was a momentous announcement indeed, for it marked the beginning of the fuel-oil period in the history of petroleum, a period that would last from 1900 to 1910 and would make fuel-oil production one of the richest business bonanzas in the country.

As the demand for oil rose sharply, another round of frenzied drilling took place on Spindletop, the new and more dazzling name for Big Hill. By the end of the year five

8 W. P. A. Federal Writers' Project, *Beaumont: A Guide to the City and Its Environs*, 103.

hundred derricks, some of them with two or more wells operating under their platforms, were tangled together on 144 acres of land, as scores of rival companies pumped out a staggering total of 1,750,000 barrels of crude oil and shipped it to industrial centers all over the world. "Beaumont oil," observed a happy oil man, "is burning in Germany, England, Cuba, Mexico, New York and Philadelphia. By its energy steamers are being propelled across the ocean, trains are hastening across the continent, electricity generated and artificial ice frozen in New York, ores ground and stamped in Mexico, Portland cement manufactured in Havana and Texas, and gas enriched in Philadelphia."[9] In less than a year, a sandy dome in the marshes south of Beaumont had made the United States the leading oil-producing nation in the world.

Beaumonters looked on all this like visitors at some spectacle, not quite sure what to think of the revolutionary changes taking place around them. As promoters and lease men came knocking at their doors, offering them fantastic sums of money for their property, some Beaumonters became rich beyond their wildest dreams. A commissary clerk who had recently bought four acres of land for $60 now sold it for $100,000. An illiterate old woman was persuaded to part with her pig farm for $35,000. A Negro dirt farmer who had been away on a visit when the boom began was stunned speechless by the thronging scene which greeted him on his return. Beaumont's streets, swarming with twenty to thirty thousand "boomers," were virtually impassable. Speculators stood on every street corner, peddling stock in oil companies like barkers at a carnival. Street urchins sold whisky bottles full of oil at a dollar each; and a hack-

[9] R. T. Hill, "The Beaumont Oil Field, with Notes on Other Oil Fields of the Texas Region," *Journal of the Franklin Institute*, (August–October, 1902), 26.

man charged sightseers (as many as 15,000 in one day) eighteen dollars apiece to haul them from the depot—a veritable ant bed of activity—out to Spindletop. Here and there in the milling crowds ear-ringed women could be seen offering a different ware for sale.

The Negro farmer might well have thought he was in the wrong town. This was sleepy little Beaumont, where time had stood as still as a windless summer day? As he headed his wagon homeward, he met a white man who offered him $20,000 for his place. The Negro, who'd been trying to sell it for $150 for three years, looked at the man incredulously —*twenty thousand dollars?* When the man nodded, the Negro took his check before he changed his mind, and might have shouted for joy had he not encountered another man farther on who offered him $50,000 for the farm—in cash. Just then the new owner came up and sold it to the second fellow for a $30,000 profit in the space of fifteen minutes.[10]

And so it went throughout the first year of the boom, as lease men representing hundreds of companies fanned out over the countryside paying anywhere from $1,000 to $1,000,000 an acre for farm and pasture land. Local farmers who sold their property for prices like that at first did not know what to do with themselves. What did one do when one had worked ten to fourteen hours a day, six days a week, for twenty years? When one was used to eating cornbread and bacon twice a day and wearing overalls and soiled denim shirts? Most of them, like the woman who sold her pig farm, continued to live precisely as they had before, buying a small place in town or even another farm far away from the oil field, regarding their money as little more than an oddity, something to talk about with their neighbors on the porch on warm Sunday afternoons.

[10] Clark and Halbouty, *Spindletop*, 75–76; Rister, *Oil!*, 61–62.

The boom affected everyone in Beaumont, even those who owned no land and bought no stock in the oil companies operating there. Businesses of all kinds—cafés, barber shops, hotels, mercantile stores—did a thriving trade, as the population exploded from 10,000 to 50,000 in four months. Lawyers made small fortunes handling scores of lawsuits and disputes over leases. And bankers were starry-eyed, noting with uninhibited happiness that oil and leasing companies had already invested $4,371,085 in oil activities and had deposited, by July, 1901, a total of $3,369,587 in all Beaumont banks, including two new ones. By the end of the year, Beaumont could boast that it had more money and more "locomobiles and automobiles" than any place else in "the whole state of Texas." The Beaumont *Enterprise* burbled: "We are independent of everybody and everything. We are wealthy beyond our calculations."[11]

But if the boom brought unprecedented prosperity to Beaumont, it also brought trouble. For one thing, with waste oil lying in open lakes around Spindletop and with all the careless, irresponsible drilling going on there with spark-throwing steam engines, giant fires periodically broke out. One burned up sixty-two derricks, with sheets of flame and black oil smoke leaping a thousand feet into the sky. From a housetop in Beaumont, the hill at night looked like Dante's Hell, and there was fearful speculation that the fire might spread into town. But at last it was brought under control. After that the oil companies adopted safety measures to prevent any more conflagrations, and set about burning waste oil, digging proper drainage systems, ordering their workers to stay sober on the job, and keeping road-side saloons away from the oil field. But even with these precautions, Beaumonters lived in constant fear that a fire would

11 Beaumont *Enterprise*, August 20, 1901.

rage out of control, sweep across the oil-soaked land, and consume the town itself in a ghastly holocaust.[12]

For another thing, Beaumont's cistern water was unpotable. Doctors told people to drink whisky or boiled water, but thousands of boomers and natives drank the bad water anyway. This led to epidemics of diarrhea which prospectors called "the Beaumonts," and diarrhea in turn led to other difficulties. Hospital and medical facilities were virtually nonexistent. Beaumont's sewage system, if it can be called that, was "almost medieval," consisting of drainage ditches, private outhouses, and a half-dozen public two-seaters behind Crosby's Bar. At any time day or night one could find fifty to a hundred men suffering from the Beaumonts gathered there. Young Beaumont boys made as high as ten dollars a day lining up and selling their places as they neared the outhouses. But some sufferers could not wait, and were forced to relieve themselves in alleys and narrow passageways. This, in turn, attracted hordes of flies—the same flies that would infest people's homes and crawl over uncovered food in nearby sidewalk and greasy spoon cafés. Until the city provided better water facilities and constructed an adequate sewage system, epidemics of the flu and other diseases would sweep unchecked through Beaumont.

Then there was the polluted air—Beaumont may in fact have been the first American city to suffer from that malady. Gas hissed out of Spindletop's wells—there was no attempt to control it—and drifted in over the city, forming gas pockets around houses and in the streets which could blow people to pieces if they struck a match or the headlights on their automobiles fatefully spluttered. There were also oil fogs, caused primarily by the gushers, which lay over the

---

[12] Rister, *Oil!*, 62; Clark and Halbouty, *Spindletop*, 94–96; and Boyce House, *Oil Boom*, 85. House creates an especially vivid picture of the fires which periodically ravaged Spindletop and of social conditions in Beaumont during the boom.

city like a ghostly pall when the air was still, turning houses yellow and keeping residents awake all night coughing from the stench. Even on clear, windy days the odor of gas and crude oil was often so strong that people who went outside had to cover their noses with handkerchiefs.[13]

Then, to add another dimension to Beaumont's troubles, there were hundreds of ruthless bogus stock promoters operating all over the city. They worked in the open, in saloons and cafés and lobbies of respectable hotels, high-pressuring speculators—or naïve Beaumont natives who wanted to invest their savings in a money-making venture—into buying stock in their "million dollar" oil companies. How much did these tricksters take? Nobody knows for certain, but the following figures might give one an idea: eight months after the Lucas gusher, capitalization of Texas oil companies alone had climbed to $231 million, yet only $11 million had actually been invested in the field. Moreover, by the end of 1901 some 585 companies were allegedly operating on 244 acres at the Spindletop field. Four of these companies, capitalized at a million dollars apiece, held a joint lease on a forty-five-foot lot while brokers sold their stock for fabulous prices in town. It was no wonder that people who were robbed by such fraudulent stock companies bitterly changed the oil field's name to Swindletop.[14]

Beaumont was swarming with other kinds of human parasites too—with cardsharps, dope peddlers, pickpockets, hijackers, fortune tellers, single girls looking for big-time spenders, professional gunslingers, racketeers, saloon and dance-hall entrepreneurs, and a veritable army of white and Negro prostitutes. Crockett Street—or Deep Crockett—became the haven for these people, and within a few months it had the reputation of being the most notorious red-light dis-

13 Clark and Halbouty, *Spindletop*, 85.
14 Mody C. Boatright, *Folklore of the Oil Industry*, 97.

trict in the United States. For oil-field workers who wanted action after a grueling day on Spindletop, Deep Crockett was the place to go. Here streetwalkers were as common as flies. Brothels were located over every saloon, gambling "joint," and dance hall. At one "vaudeville house," the girls advertised themselves on the balcony, stripping to honky-tonk music and dancing out risqué and lascivious acts to tease those who needed teasing into making a "date." Men who did so got five minutes of hired love on a cot in a back-room cubbyhole.

In time satellite tent and shack cities went up around the oil field itself, and fresh waves of harlots passed through Beaumont and took up residence there. The Deep Crockett girls, seldom lacking in competitiveness, took to riding out to the oil field on horseback, offering themselves at special rates and turning their houses over to crews of men—on a sort of group plan—for whole nights at a time.[15]

Then there were the diseases—the price men paid for the satisfaction of their needs. There were also the drunken brawls all over the Beaumont area, the knife fights, hold-ups, beatings, and finally the murders, which occurred "so frequently," lamented the Beaumont *Enterprise,* that "they have ceased to excite more than ordinary interest."[16]

What did the police do to combat the crime wave? The police and sheriff's departments were both so understaffed and underpaid that all the harried police chief could do was to issue warnings to the townspeople. Stay in your homes at night, he told them, and keep your doors locked. If you have to go out, walk in the middle of the street. And "tote your guns," he added, "and tote 'em in your hands, so everybody can see you're loaded."[17] But in time even the police were

[15] Clark and Halbouty, *Spindletop,* 83–84, 97.

[16] Quoted in W. P. A. Federal Writers' Project, *Beaumont,* 113.

[17] *Ibid.,* 104.

afraid to go out after dark, and Beaumont became a surreal-istic nightmare of vice and murder.

After two years of unchecked violence, Beaumont citizens decided to take matters into their own hands. On the night of May 7, 1903, a thousand men and "a sprinkling of ladies" met at the new Kyle Opera House (itself a product of the boom) and organized a Citizens' Law and Order League with the support of the Beaumont Oil Exchange and Board of Trade. In the weeks that followed, this committee, threat-ening to resort to "a few legal hangings" if it had to, purged Beaumont of a large number of "undesirables" and closed down many of the brothels and "joints" in Deep Crockett.[18]

But what finally brought an end to Beaumont's lawless-ness was the demise of the oil field itself. In 1902, the year of peak production, Spindletop had yielded 17,420,949 barrels of oil, but by 1904 production had fallen off to scarcely 10,000 barrels a day. One by one the companies and their armies of workers moved on to Oklahoma, where new fields had been discovered around Tulsa. When the oil-field workers left, so did the whores, the swindlers, dope peddlers, hijackers, and all the other rogues who lived on the lusts and ignorances of men.

By 1924, Spindletop was nearly abandoned. A few run-down buildings were all that remained of Gladys City. Junked wagons, oily wooden storage tanks, abandoned rigs, and joints of rusted pipe lay around like debris on a long-forgotten battlefield. There was still a pungent odor of sulfur gas and oil, grisly reminders of the inordinate waste that had accompanied the boom. There was also, if one listened closely, the familiar metallic screech of sucker rods and the muted concussion of pump jacks, as a few die-hard com-panies drew the last trickles of oil out of Spindletop. But in time even they were gone. Then a silence lay over the aban-

18 *Ibid.*, 113.

doned field, a silence broken only by an occasional swarm of birds.

There was a kind of silence in Beaumont, too, rather like that which follows a violent storm. With the exodus of oil men and their camp followers to Oklahoma, the population had shrunk to 20,000, mostly merchants, white-collar workers, and former promoters who had no place else to go. Life had slowed down too, as people gradually went back to doing what they had done before. Captain Lucas gave up drilling for oil and went into consultant engineering. Patillo Higgins and a future oil magnate named E. L. DeGolyer were poring over maps of the coast—might there not be oil under some of these other salt domes?—and Higgins was again becoming the subject of street-corner gossip, though not with quite the same sarcasm as before. Scores of other oil men who had lost every dime they had when the field dried up, could now be found washing dishes in local chili houses, digging ditches, or panhandling on street corners.[19]

But Beaumont had not seen the last of the oil boom. In 1925 the Yount-Lee Oil Company, drilling down 2,588 feet under Spindletop, found another huge oil reservoir. The Beaumont area boomed again, but this time the large oil companies jointly controlled all oil-field operations so that there was little of the frenzied speculation and irresponsible drilling that had characterized the first boom. Also, the city fathers, backed up by an enlarged police force, ran a tight orderly town, chasing out whatever riffraff tried to come in. The second boom thus had all the economic advantages of the first and little of its degradation and violence. Thanks to the millions of dollars that again poured into Beaumont, city planners were able to construct such badly needed facilities as a $500,000 hospital and several bright new schools.

[19] DeGolyer, "Anthony F. Lucas and Spindletop," *Southwest Review*, XXXI, 86–87; and Clark and Halbouty, *Spindletop*, 215, 251.

In addition, construction companies erected six new banks, dozens of new stores and office buildings, and two sky-scraping hotels that shone brilliantly against the Texas sun. By 1929 the greater Beaumont area was the center of a vast industrial empire, with six refineries, a nexus of giant pipe-lines that ran to Port Arthur and Houston (which had also grown prodigiously from the boom), and an enlarged ship channel which gave Beaumont all the facilities of a modern port.[20] Thus, thanks to a couple of clear-eyed and stubborn individuals named Patillo Higgins and Anthony Lucas, what once had been a backward little Southern sawmill town had grown into a twentieth-century industrial metropolis—the first in the Southwest built by oil money.

But the significance of Spindletop—of the clear-eyed vision of Higgins and Lucas—was not limited just to the Beaumont area. The great oil field also had a profound impact on the nation at large. Not only had it produced more wealth, for all sorts of business activities, than the California Gold Rush of 1848–49; Spindletop had also given birth to such titans of the petroleum industry as Gulf Oil Company, Humble, Sun Oil Company, and the Texas Company, whose worldwide operations finally had broken the monopoly of the American oil market which Standard Oil had enjoyed for decades. But most important of all, Spindletop had launched the United States into a new era—the oil and gasoline age, an age that would shape her national character and direct her industrial energies for a full half-century.

[20] Rister, *Oil!*, 230.

VII

The Space Age
Comes
to the
Southwest

HE Houston area emerged from the oil boom with an image that became almost as widely known—and perhaps just as shrouded with myths, thanks to motion pictures like *Giant*—as that of the Old West cow towns. *Houston* meant *oil*, just as Dodge City some eighty years earlier had meant cow herds and cowboys. By 1960, with a metropolitan population of 1,251,700, a $3 billion oil and petrochemical industry, a $68 million ship channel, and skyscraping oil-company office buildings that stood as symbols of the oil man's energy and productiveness, Houston was incontestibly the oil capital of the Southwest, if not of all the United States west of the Mississippi.[1]

On September 19, 1961, however, James E. Webb of the National Aeronautics and Space Administration made a momentous announcement at Washington, D.C., that promised to alter the image of Greater Houston as largely an oil industry phenomenon. NASA, Webb said, had selected Houston over some twenty other cities as the site for a new manned spacecraft center that would be the command post for the nation's space program. NASA would build the center on a

[1] *Houston Magazine*, September, 1962, p. 28.

little-known tract of land bordering Clear Lake, some twenty-two miles southeast of downtown Houston, and would include in the facility a multimillion-dollar flight control headquarters to direct Project Apollo—a three-man, round-trip rocket flight to the moon, scheduled for around 1970.

For the Houston area, NASA's announcement portended new dimensions in scientific and technological growth. "This is Wonderful News," headlined a *Houston Magazine* feature story. The space center would, it believed, start an economic boom comparable to that associated with the oil rush and with the opening of the ship channel back in 1915.[2] Businessmen, anticipating new developments in the technical commercial areas, were especially elated over NASA's choice, and the Chamber of Commerce went so far as to proclaim it "the most significant single event" in the city's rich economic history.[3] Soon there was a heady effect on the populace like that of the oil boom days as professional men also began to talk in superlatives about the coming of the Manned Spacecraft Center; educators and university scientists even predicted that it would bring to Houston some of the most brilliant minds in the nation. "Placing such talent and equipment here," said University of Houston President Philip Hoffman, "can only have a beneficial effect."[4] Across the Greater Houston area, men of every economic and social station looked to the future with alacrity and high hopes. "NASA," quipped a paper in upstate Dallas, "has put Houston in orbit."[5]

NASA's decision to move to Houston came rather abruptly, after a few short weeks of studying the city's scientific

[2] *Ibid.*, October, 1961, p. 68. See United Press International in Dallas *Herald*, September 19, 1961, for a news release of Webb's announcement and for a discussion of how Houston's industry influenced NASA's decision.

[3] Dallas *Herald*, September 19, 1961.

[4] Associated Press in Wichita Falls *Times*, October 12, 1961.

[5] Dallas *Morning News*, April 22, 1962. See also issue of September 20, 1961.

and industrial potential. But, in a broader sense, the decision grew out of a swift series of space events that began back on October 4, 1957, when the Soviet Union launched man's first satellite into orbit around the earth. Though Sputnik was the work of a totalitarian power, scientists over the world, rising above nationality and political commitment, saw in its small dimensions not only the accumulated brilliance of man, but also the beginning of a new era in history—the Age of Space. In terms of the balance of power, though, this 184-pound sphere spinning through the heavens started a nervous shiver down the spine of the free world. The United States, of course, reacted with shock and outraged pride. The Eisenhower Administration moved quickly to disparage Sputnik as a clever propaganda stunt without military implication, but others on these shores viewed it as a stunning blow to the nation's prestige which had come about largely because of America's lagging educational system, with its undertrained teachers and uninspired pupils. This public furor later reached the boiling point when Wernher von Braun, head of the army's Redstone missile program, told Congress that, had the Administration authorized him, he could have put a United States satellite into orbit back in 1956. The tide of criticism, rising higher, soon created a political situation which the Eisenhower Administration wanted clearly to counteract, and it proceeded with a crash program designed to launch an American satellite as soon as possible. But unfortunately for the nation, the program degenerated into a feud among the three military services, each with a rocket project underway, over which one should launch the satellite. At last, on January 31, 1958, after embarrassing mishaps with two navy Vanguard rockets, after Russia orbited another Sputnik, this one with a live dog on board, von Braun and the army restored some of the nation's prestige by sending a 30.9-pound sphere called Explorer I into orbit.[6]

After that the military services competed viciously for funds to fire rockets and orbit satellites. Such interservice rivalry wasted minds and money and accomplished little. Soon one thing was glaringly obvious: if the United States was to overcome the growing gap between its space program and that of the Soviet Union, then a single space agency must be created to co-ordinate the military, the aerospace industry, and the various scientific organizations engaged in rocket research. The government took a giant step in this direction in July, 1958, when Congress passed the National Space Act, a measure that subsequently set up the National Aeronautics and Space Administration.[7] That October the new civilian agency organized itself around the National Advisory Committee for Aeronautics, a forty-three-year-old aeronautical research organizaton whose 8,040-man staff enjoyed a reputation for exceptional technical competence. NASA then transferred the various military programs under its own supervision; the Department of Defense promptly offered its unqualified support; and as a result the nation's space program moved ahead under the direction of one co-ordinating, decision-making, civilian body, whose space activities would be "devoted to peaceful purpose for the benefit of all mankind."[8]

On October 7—a little more than a year after Sputnik I— NASA announced a man-in-space venture called Project

[6] Jay Holmes, *America on the Moon: The Enterprise of the 60's*, 37–70. Other writings that will enlighten one on America's rocket and satellite programs are Loyd S. Swenson, Jr., James M. Grimwood, and Charles C. Alexander, *This New Ocean: A History of Project Mercury*; Robert Jastrow (ed.), *The Exploration of Space*; and Willy Ley, *Rockets, Missiles, and Space Travel*.

[7] Alison E. Griffith, *The Genesis of the National Aeronautics and Space Act of 1958*.

[8] Eugene M. Emme, *Historical Origins of National Aeronautics and Space Administration* (NASA Fact Sheet #110), 2–5.

Mercury. Consisting of two phases, ballistics or suborbital flights followed by orbital flights, the Mercury program would provide critical data on man's capabilities in a space environment and would perfect rocketry for subsequent missions into outer space. To carry out this project, NASA organized a Space Task Group at Langley Field, Hampton, Virginia—an organization that would later make up the manned spacecraft team at Houston. Then NASA proceeded to select seven of the country's best military test pilots for astronaut training and to give McDonnell Aircraft of St. Louis a contract for the space capsule.

Through the next two years Project Mercury bogged in a storm of criticism, excess publicity, and inexplicable technical failures in the rocket boosters. Then, in the spring of 1961, several events occurred in rapid-fire sequence that brought a radical change in Mercury's efficiency and overall objectives and that led ultimately to NASA's move to Houston. The first event happened on April 12, 1961: on that day Russia put the first man into space—a Red airforce pilot named Yuri Gagarin, whose single orbit around the globe was clothed in a dark veil of totalitarian secrecy. Still, Gagarin's flight was a spectacular achievement which dealt America's international prestige perhaps the most severe blow it had yet sustained. Clearly the United States had to do something. But what? Newly elected President John F. Kennedy, caught in the confusing change of administrations, could only call on the nation to stand by the colors and pressure NASA to try a suborbital flight and soon. Accordingly, on May 5, 1961, a von Braun Redstone rocket boosted a Mercury capsule with Alan B. Shepard, Jr., on board into a five-minute voyage in space. Shepard's flight, though hardly comparable to Gagarin's, nevertheless restored the nation's confidence in the Mercury program, in the whole broad philosophy of manned space exploration.

Consequently, twenty days later, President Kennedy delivered to Congress an epic declaration that made Project Mercury and subsequent missions a major instrument of national policy. The United States, to ensure its future on earth, to retain its leading role in peaceful scientific progress, must beat the Russians into the heavens; the United States must, Kennedy declared, commit itself to a manned flight to the moon by 1970. After mild debate, Congress endorsed the moon mission with a virtual blank check. And the United States started forward on the boldest enterprise it had ever undertaken.[9]

The accelerated program began with NASA's announcement that the moon shot would consist of three phases: one-man flights up to three days (Project Mercury); two-man flights to develop the rendezvous and docking techniques necessary for the moon flight (Project Gemini); and the lunar mission itself (Project Apollo). To accomplish all of these by 1970, NASA had to reorganize and re-establish its scattered space agencies. First it created the Office of Manned Space Flight at Washington to co-ordinate the entire program, then sent teams of experts over the country in search of suitable places for space centers and rocket factories. The result was a virtually new space complex whose component parts, though situated in the South, would draw on industrial and scientific communities over the nation. In the new complex, Cape Canaveral would continue as the actual launching site; the Marshall Space Flight Center at Huntsville, Alabama, would develop the moon rockets, building them at the Michoud Ordnance Plant near New Orleans and testing them near the Pearl River in southeastern Mississippi; and a manned spacecraft center at Houston would act as the actual command post for all space opera-

[9] Holmes, *America on the Moon*, 70–94; Loyd S. Swenson, Jr., "The Fertile Crescent: the South's Role in the National Space Program," *Southwestern Historical Quarterly*, LXXI (January, 1968), 382–83.

tions. The nucleus of the Houston center, which was to be operational by early 1964, would be the Space Task Group at Langley Field, Virginia. The center would have multiple tasks to perform: it would serve as the management agency to work out the nation's space plans and to contract with American industry for the necessary hardware, and it would design and test the space vehicles, train the astronauts, and direct flights after lift-off from Cape Canaveral. On the success or failure of the Houston headquarters to accomplish these things would rest the destiny of the United States and of the entire free world.[10]

NASA chose Houston over other cities such as Boston, Los Angeles, New Orleans, and Jacksonville, Florida, for a variety of reasons.[11] One, to be sure, was the political pressure that Texans holding key positions in the federal government brought to bear. Congressman Albert Thomas of Houston, for example, was chairman of the House Appropriations Subcommittee which handled NASA's funds—a position that allowed Thomas to become a veritable one-man lobby for his home city. Vice-President Lyndon B. Johnson, as chairman of the National Space Committee, also had some influence on NASA's choice.[12] But the truly deciding factor was not political pressure; it was the winning combination of advantages which Houston itself had to offer. Chief among these was the fact that Houston's ship channel and port facilities, which moved more tonnage than any seaport in the

[10] Emme, *Historical Origins of National Aeronautics and Space Administration*, 8–10; Elwyn H. Yeater, *The NASA Spacecraft Center and Its Programs* (NASA Fact Sheet #112), 1–3; Paul E. Purser, *The Scope of the NASA Research Laboratory at Clear Lake, Texas*, 2.

[11] NASA site selection teams also considered the following Texas cities: El Paso, Dallas, Corpus Christi, Beaumont, Victoria, Liberty, and Harlingen. NASA ruled them out because they lacked either port facilities or strong supporting industry. James M. Grimwood, Historian, Manned Spacecraft Center, to S. B. O., Houston, interview, July 22, 1963. See also Dallas *Morning News*, August 24, 1961.

[12] Houston *Chronicle*, September 24, 27, 1961; *Houston Magazine*, October, 1961, p. 68.

nation except New York, provided an excellent means of transporting bulky space vehicles to other NASA locations, especially to Cape Canaveral. Other advantages, in their order of importance, were Houston's mighty industrial complex whose manufacturies and refineries, producing 38.6 per cent of the nation's oil-tool capacity, 32 per cent of its petroleum, and about 75 per cent of its petrochemicals, were capable of expanding—of adding depth and dimension in electronics and aerospace fields—to support a space center; the scientific and research facilities available at Rice University, the University of Houston, and the Texas Medical Center; Houston's vast repository of engineers and skilled craftsmen and its 550,730-man labor force; a temperate climate that permitted year-round work; some 1,000 acres of land, donated by Rice University, for the installation of the space center; the Houston International Airport which provided first-class, all-weather jet service to strategic places in the United States and beyond; and finally the city's recreational and cultural assets such as the Houston Symphony Society, the Houston Museum of Fine Arts, and six professional and civic theaters.[13] None of the other communities NASA considered could offer such advantages for the headquarters of a crash program designed to lead the world into outer space.

Its reorganization completed, NASA started construction at once at Clear Lake. It gave the United States Army Corps of Engineers from the Fort Worth District the job of supervising all construction operations, then negotiated contracts for the work itself. Soon bulldozers and other heavy machinery belonging to Morrison-Knudsen Company of Boise,

---

[13] James Stafford, "Behind the NASA Move to Houston," *Texas Business Review*, XXXVI, (April, 1962), 90–94; "First Year: Space-Age Impact on Houston," *Houston Magazine*, September, 1962, pp. 28–31. This article includes the "14 Points" which NASA used in choosing a location for the permanent Manned Spacecraft Center.

Idaho, and Paul Hardeman, Inc., of Los Angeles rumbled onto the Clear Lake site to grade, build roads, and set up water and power systems for the projected space center. After these came teams of engineers and architects from Brown and Root, Inc., a Houston firm which won the $1.5 million contract to design the center's main building complex.[14] By the spring of 1962, over two thousand workmen and scores of roaring machines moved like large ants over a tract of land that only a few months earlier had been an open prairie along the shores of Clear Lake, hitherto an insignificant body of water that in the distance opened into Galveston Bay.

Since the new center would not be ready until April, 1964, NASA decided to lease temporary facilities inside Houston and carry on its space program there. In late May, 1962, a few days after John Glenn became the first American to orbit the earth, NASA began the exacting move from Langley— a move that proved even more difficult than expected since the scientists and technicians there, 1,152 in number, were mostly civilians who could not be ordered to Houston. To remove their doubts about transferring, the Houston Chamber of Commerce—"this was something we wanted, and we went out for it"—sent representatives to Langley loaded with two hundred pounds of propaganda about Houston's cultural and economic assets.[15] They were quite persuasive, too, since all but eighty-four employees elected to make the change and started packing.[16] By July 1, 1962, a little over a month after Scott Carpenter's three-orbit flight, the last

[14] To meet its construction deadline, Brown & Root promptly hired a group called Associated Architects to help. This organization consisted of Austin architects Brooks & Barr and Houston architectural firms of Mackie & Kamrath; Harvey C. Moore; and Wirtz, Calhoun, Tungate, & Jackson. *Houston Magazine*, September, 1962, p. 27. See also issue of May, 1962, p. 23.

[15] Howard N. Martin, Manager of Research Department, Houston Chamber of Commerce, to S. B. O., Houston, interview, August 2, 1963; Associated Press in Dallas *Herald*, November 27, 1961.

[16] Grimwood to S. B. O., Houston, interview, July 22, 1963.

member of the spacecraft team had arrived in Houston. The next day the nation's seventh largest metropolis took on a new title: "Space City, U.S.A."[17]

All this called for celebrations, and the Chamber of Commerce announced plans for a huge welcome parade "in the best Houston tradition" for July 4. At mid-morning a thirty-six-car parade started off from the Sam Houston Coliseum, with a wailing police escort in front, followed by the astronauts and their families, then by several hundred NASA engineers and scientists and "other Space Age celebrities" like Congressman Albert Thomas, and finally by a genuine Mercury spacecraft, mounted on a special trailer. Around and through downtown Houston curled the long, black line of convertibles, whose celebrated passengers waved at thousands of Houstonians along the streets who cheered and waved back. At last the motorcade came again to the Coliseum and halted, and the herd of celebrities and guests— five thousand of them—swept inside, into cavernous Exhibit Hall for speeches and a mass barbecue. Almost everyone of note, it seemed, gave a talk that sweltering day—Chamber of Commerce officials, politicians, the mayor. After them came Robert R. Gilruth, director of the Manned Spacecraft Center, an expert in hypersonic aerodynamics, to explain what the center would do in Houston; his deputy director, Walter C. Williams, and his special assistant, Paul E. Purser, each gave a few remarks, then turned the microphone over to "The Voice of Mercury Control" himself, Colonel John "Shorty" Powers, who introduced the seven astronauts to the applauding crowd. Then while resplendent school bands played high and shrill, the gathering became a sea of eating, chattering faces. An hour later it was all over, and all the Texans, every one of them, astronauts and scientists included, left with the knowledge that it had been "the most

17 "Houston Welcomes MSC," *Houston Magazine*, August, 1962, p. 26.

meaningful Fourth of July parade that Houston has had in recent times."[18]

The next day an eager team of NASA personnel resumed their work on Project Mercury at twelve different offices and laboratories scattered over the city and at several renovated barracks out at Ellington Field. There was much to be done. The long move from Langley had consumed valuable time— time that had to be made up if Americans were to land on the moon within eight short years and do so before the Russians. Also, another Mercury flight—a six-orbit affair—was scheduled for the next fall, which meant that the spacecraft must be improved, the support systems tested, and the astronauts vigorously trained. At the same time, work must continue on the Gemini and Apollo missions, as well as on such infinitely more advanced projects as an orbiting space station, a lunar base, and manned flights to other planets. These, in turn, required more astronauts, more scientists and technicians, and more contracts with industry for the necessary space equipment. It all meant, in short, that the Manned Spacecraft Center had to work virtually through light and darkness and do it in a vortex of confusion—the inevitable disarray that comes when such a large enterprise tries to carry on in new and haphazard facilities.[19]

In its initial months at Houston, the Manned Spacecraft Center concentrated primarily on two things—letting contracts for the Gemini and Apollo projects and preparing for the Mercury voyage that fall. After considerable negotiation, MSC at last gave contracts to McDonnell Aircraft, already building the Mercury capsules, for the Gemini vehicle; to North American Aviation of Downey, California, for most of the Apollo spacecraft; to the Massachusetts Institute of

---

[18] *Ibid.*, 26–35; Houston *Post*, July 5, 1962.

[19] Yeater, *The NASA Manned Spacecraft Center and Its Programs*, 3–4; Maxime A. Faget, *Engineering and Scientific Goals of the NASA Manned Space Flight Program* (NASA Fact Sheet #125), 1–10.

Technology for Apollo's navigation and control systems; to Grumman Aircraft of Long Island for the Lunar Excursion Module, a bug-like machine in which two of the three Apollo pilots would land on the moon; and to numerous other aerospace firms for individual computer and electronic systems. The cost of these "prime" contracts was astronomical, over one billion dollars, which was perhaps more than the nation would have liked to spend.[20] Nevertheless, such staggering expenditures were to be expected since, as one MSC official pointed out, "the real cost of the space program is not mass production of spacecraft or boosters, but, as you see, is spent in developing specialized equipment" which required enormous expense for basic research.[21]

While negotiations for other contracts continued, the Manned Spacecraft Center transferred its huge 7094 electronic computer—"the brain" which would analyze space data and monitor the progress of the space capsules—from Langley to temporary facilities at the University of Houston.[22] After that, the various technical departments preoccupied themselves with the tedious business of testing equipment and procedure for the forthcoming orbital flight. As they did so, the heavy summer heat began to wane and turned at last into autumn. The focus of NASA shifted then from the Houston center to Cape Canaveral, only to shift back abruptly when President Kennedy announced plans to inspect the major NASA installations, including MSC, within a week. Quickly, MSC workers tidied up their offices and

[20] *Project Gemini Fact Sheet*, 3–5; Robert R. Gilruth, *Interview With Data Magazine* (NASA Fact Sheet #114), 3; *Houston Magazine*, March, 1963, pp. 26, 28. North America's contract alone was $319,922,328—the largest NASA had awarded to date.

[21] Dave W. Lang, Purchase Request for the Moon (typescript, photostatic copy in possession of the author), 3. This manuscript was a prepared statement which Lang, chief of the Manned Spacecraft Center's Procurements and Contracts Division, read at a Press Conference at MSC site 9, Houston, July 26, 1963. See also Houston *Chronicle*, July 26, 1963.

[22] *Houston Magazine*, August, 1962, p. 25.

labs while public relations men organized with city officials another welcome parade and called on Houstonians to turn out en masse. On the evening of September 11, the President flew in from New Orleans, rode triumphantly through downtown Houston, through a blizzard of ticker tape and cheering throngs of citizens, and came at last to the Rice Hotel for speeches and press conferences and for late-evening entertainment. The next morning he got down to business. He toured MSC's facilities and got a closed briefing on NASA's space work to date, then rode away to Rice Stadium to tell some fifty thousand people there about America's space objectives and what these portended for Houston and the Greater Bay area. Standing under a bright, blazing sun, looking out over his audience, Kennedy started speaking in his clipped Boston accent. During the next five years, he said, "your city will become the heart of a large scientific and engineering community." In that time, "the National Aeronautics and Space Administration expects to double the number of scientists and engineers in this area—to increase its outlays for salaries and expenses to $60 Million a year —to invest some $200 Million here in plant and laboratory facilities—and to direct or contract for new space efforts at a rate of $1 Billion a year from this space center alone."

The audience interrupted him with a thundering applause; over the months the citizens there had heard about such figures, but until then had not really thought about them in terms of what they meant for the Houston economy. "Outer space is there," the President continued. "The moon and the planets beyond are there—new hopes for knowledge and peace are there with them." Again the audience clapped, but Kennedy went on, his right arm pumping slightly, to declare that "If we are, my fellow citizens, to send to the moon, 240,000 miles away from the control station here in Houston, a giant rocket more than 300 feet high—made of new alloys that have not yet even been developed—capable of standing heats and stresses several times that ever before experienced—fitted together with a precision many times finer than the finest watch—carrying all the equipment needed for propulsion, guidance, control, communications, food and survival on an untried mission to an unknown celestial body—and then return it safely to earth, re-entering the atmosphere at speeds up to 25,000 miles an hour, causing heat about half the temperature of the sun—almost as hot as it is here today—and do all this and do it right and do it first before this decade is out—then we must be bold and daring and unflinching."

When he was through moments later, fifty thousand Houstonians rose to give him a standing ovation, then left the stadium with a fierce sense of a new manifest destiny—an intrinsic human right to explore and to conquer the farthest limits of their solar system. Even the NASA men, who themselves had heard and given similar speeches before, walked away that day with a clearer understanding of what was possible. And all knew, then, that the Space Age was irrevocably here, in their midst, and that their lives as well as those of their children after them would be vastly changed by it.[23]

As it turned out, the President's visit proved enormously beneficial to MSC's work in Houston. His speech, his very presence, stirred the populace there to a new and greater awareness of America's space program. And this growing public consciousness, in turn, gave the space team itself a higher understanding of its own responsibilities. Thus when Walter M. Schirra, Jr., on October 3, 1962, rode an Atlas rocket into a six-orbit journey in space, when Houston afterwards billed him as its first citizen in space and gave him a rousing "welcome home" reception, the Manned Spacecraft Center decided to expand a program begun the previous

[23] Houston *Post*, September 13, 1962. See also Dallas *Morning News*, September 13, 1962.

summer to keep the community apprised of its progress and its achievements. Led by Eugene E. Horton, head of MSC's Community Relations Branch, top NASA officials literally saturated the South Texas area with space talks; they spoke to college and university audiences, to PTA meetings, to business and professional groups, and to gatherings of the press. Then they branched out, over the state, holding space forums in virtually every major city from the Gulf Coast to the far-away Panhandle. The idea behind all of these talks was to give the people of Texas a better scientific understanding of the nation's space conquests and to explain "who we are, why we are here, and what we are doing."[24]

At the same time, the space center brought to Houston a NASA spacemobile—one of ten operating over the country —which was little more than a truck that contained displays of rockets and other space paraphernalia. This spacemobile had already been to Houston once, the previous August, and had proved tremendously effective in displaying its contents to the Harris County Teachers Workshop. On its second visit that December the spacemobile went to every Houston school, where its driver, an accomplished speaker named Joe Anctil, bewitched the students with graphic descriptions of a rocket trip to the moon.[25]

After L. Gordon Cooper's successful twenty-two-orbit flight in the spring of 1963, the Manned Spacecraft Center tried other means of perpetuating its public image. It began to hold official tours for educational groups, guiding them through its space laboratories, showing them slides, and taking them by bus to the Clear Lake site. Then, at the new Houston World Trade Center, MSC set up a permanent exhibit designed to inform foreign visitors and technical and educational groups about the expanding programs of the

[24] Eugene E. Horton, Manned Spacecraft Center, to S. B. O., Houston, interview, July 22, 1963.

[25] *Ibid.*; *Houston Magazine*, August, 1962, p. 25.

National Aeronautics and Space Administration. The display contained models of Mercury space capsules and of MSC's Clear Lake facility and had graphic charts explaining in vivid detail the Gemini and Apollo missions. Also, in an auditorium on one side of the exhibit room, MSC representatives started giving presentations to any organization that wanted more information on America's space program and MSC's growing role in it.[26]

The space center's chief aim in all this publicity was simple, yet profound. It wanted to help maintain the democratic process. For the space team readily realized that if popular government was to prevail in the age of space—an age beset with scientific and technological complexities undreamed-of before—then the people must be educated to comprehend technical issues so that they might continue to make proper and responsible decisions.[27]

There was still another reason for such wide publicity. NASA knew that it was literally making history, that it was opening "a brilliant new stage in man's evolution," and it simply wanted Houston, the Southwest, and the nation at large to recognize this.[28] It wanted the nation to know, and to know well, that America's exploration of the moon and the planets beyond "will be marked by history as one of Man's most ambitious and determined efforts" to conquer his physical universe for his own intellectual self-realization.[29]

That NASA, from its Washington office to its Manned Spacecraft Center in Houston, was aware of its role in his-

[26] *Houston Magazine*, May, 1963, p. 28.

[27] Horton to S. B. O., Houston, interview, July 22, 1963.

[28] Hugh L. Dryden, *Impact of Progress in Space on Science: Address at Joint Session of the Federation of American Societies for Experimental Biology, April 16, 1962, Atlantic City, New Jersey,* 13.

[29] Robert C. Seamans, Jr., *The National Space Program—Progress and Opportunities: Address Before the Washington Representatives Chapter of the National Security Industrial Association* (NASA Fact Sheet #111), 1.

tory was manifested in another project—the compilation of a complete written record of NASA's activities from the beginning. To do this, NASA had already established a historical branch at Washington under the direction of Eugene M. Emme. But after the reorganization in 1961, it became necessary not only to have Emme writing out of the capital, but also to have a historian or monitor at each NASA installation. Their collective task was to record America's space events almost as they happened, to provide a series of official chronicles that scholars of later generations might utilize.

The historian assigned to the Manned Spacecraft Center was a forty-year-old Albamian named James M. Grimwood. It was an excellent choice, for Grimwood had nearly a decade of experience as a government chronicler that began back in 1953, when he became the historian of the 18th Air Force. Three years later he transferred to the Air Training Command where he wrote accounts of the Titan and Thor missiles. In September, 1961, the army appointed him chief historian of its Ballistics Missile Agency at Huntsville, Alabama, and gave him the ponderous task of preparing histories of the Redstone, Pershing, and Jupiter missiles. Because of his extensive knowledge of rocketry, the government transferred him to NASA in August, 1962.[30]

As the historian of NASA's Manned Spacecraft Center, Grimwood's first assignment was to compile a chronology of Project Mercury. This was published at the center itself in 1963 and later that year was included in a five-year chronicle of NASA put out by the Government Printing Office in Washington. Then, with the help of three contract historians—Charles C. Alexander, Loyd S. Swenson, Jr., and Pamela C. Johnson, all of the University of Houston—Grimwood prepared a long, semitechnical history of Project Mer-

[30] Grimwood to S. B. O., Houston, interview, July 22, 1963.

cury called *This New Ocean* which was published at Washington.[31] Looking beyond these, Grimwood and the contract historians had considerable work ahead of them. In 1967 they would have to do a series on Project Gemini; after that, one on Project Apollo—on the incredible operations of orbiting a three-man spacecraft with a rocket whose cluster of engines would generate millions of horsepower; of boosting the craft out of its preliminary earth orbit into lunar flight; of putting it into a moon orbit while a small lunar vehicle landed and then returned to the mother ship; of firing this main craft out of the moon orbit and propelling it back across 226,971 miles into another orbit around the earth; and finally of bringing the space ship and its three pilots back to land alive and triumphant. And after that? For the historians at the Manned Spacecraft Center as well as those at other NASA installations the list of flights to write about seemed infinite—to Mars, to Jupiter, to Pluto, perhaps even to other solar systems beyond the sun.

Such future missions, however, depended entirely on the success of projects Mercury, Gemini, and Apollo. And MSC's work on these in the summer and fall of 1963 was moving rapidly on. Nine new astronauts, two of them Texans,[32] had been selected the previous October and were at last being trained to serve as crew members for the Gemini flights. At the same time, the seven Mercury astronauts, who would act as senior pilots on all voyages, were undergoing rigorous tests in full-mission simulators—huge trainers capable of producing actual space conditions. Moreover, all the astronauts were receiving extensive instruction in rocket

31 *Ibid.*; Eugene M. Emme, Administrator's Progress Report for March 1963 (typescript, photostatic copy in possession of the author).

32 Air Force Captain Edward H. White II of San Antonio and Test Pilot Elliot M. See, Jr., of Dallas were the two Texans chosen. Both were later killed. See died in a plane crash in March, 1966; and White was burned to death (with Virgil I. Grissom and Roger Chaffee) in a mishap at an Apollo launching pad at Cape Kennedy (formerly Cape Canaveral) on January 27, 1967.

propulsion, aerodynamics, astronomy, atmosphere and space physics, in environmental control systems, survival, and rendezvous and docking techniques. The primary objectives of all such training was to teach the astronauts about their spacecraft and to familiarize them with such flight conditions as acceleration, noise, heat, vibration, disorientation, and weightlessness.[33]

In the meantime, MSC had pushed ahead in other areas of flight preparation. Its scientists had made impressive gains in design and development of all forms of technical apparatus from Apollo space suits to spacecraft computer systems.[34] Recently, contracts for these and other equipment had gone out to electronics or aerospace firms. Furthermore, with MSC's expanding activities had come some two thousand new personnel—new scientists, engineers, economists, management experts, and college students participating in NASA's various internship programs—thus bringing MSC's total work force to about three thousand by August, 1963.[35]

At the same time, construction of the permanent center out at Clear Lake had proceeded at a breathtaking clip, and by the summer of 1964, NASA personnel had completed the tedious move out to the campus-like building complex. The buildings were similar in design and were functionally related, that is, arranged for maximum co-ordination and interoffice communication. They occupied perhaps 200 acres of the 1,600-acre site (NASA had added 600 acres to the original tract of land donated by Rice University); the remaining area would be used for thermonuclear test facilities and for future expansion.[36]

[33] Richard E. Day, *Flight Crew Requirements* (NASA Fact Sheet #133), 1–4; Robert B. Voas, *Astronaut Training* (NASA Fact Sheet #139), 3–5.
[34] *Project Gemini Fact Sheet*, 3–5, 16–17.
[35] Lang, Purchase Request for the Moon, 8.
[36] Joseph N. Kotanchik and H. Kurt Strass, *Test Facilities of the Manned Spacecraft Center* (NASA Fact Sheet #126), 5–6.

Of the buildings in the central complex the most impressive was the Integrated Mission Control Center—the nerve of the entire facility—which would direct all preflight and flight operations. The building itself was three stories high and was divided into an administrative wing, an interconnecting wing, and a mission operations wing, whose real-time computer system—built, installed, and maintained by International Business Machines—would analyze and process all space data coming in from the flying capsules.[37] A few yards to the southwest was another strategic facility, a central data building which housed not only computers to collect and process space information after flights, but a technical library as well; the library itself constituted a veritable space archives of papers, documents, and historical treatises. Another cluster of buildings farther to the west consisted of a multistory Project Management Office, a space research office and laboratory, and three separate facilities for systems evaluation. On the opposite end of the site, behind the Integrated Mission Control Center, stood two "outer-space silos"—environmental test chambers that subjected the astronauts and their moon craft to conditions—weightlessness and solar heating, to name two—which they would likely encounter in deep outer space. Also going up nearby, through a contract with Link Division of General Precisions Incorporated, was an Apollo-Mission Trainer in which the astronauts would be trained in such operations as first- and second-stage boost and separation, earth orbit, space parking, separation and return of the lunar landing vehicle, and finally re-entry and landing.[38] The remaining buildings in the central complex included a flight operations

[37] John D. Hodge and Tecywn Roberts, *Flight Operations Facilities* (NASA Fact Sheet #131), 4–5; *Houston Magazine*, May, 1963, p. 28; *Houston Post*, July 13, 1963.

[38] Gilruth, *Interview With Data Magazine*, 1, 8; *Houston Magazine*, July, 1963, p. 26.

181

and flight crew operations facility; research and development offices and laboratories; a flight accelerator or centrifuge; a spacecraft research building; and various support facilities such as cafeterias, a heliport, a fire station, and maintenance and technical service buildings.[39]

The Manned Spacecraft Center, as one might discern from a description of its facilities and operations, was not intended to be self-supporting. "We still depend upon the local community for housing, shopping, schools, and everything else," an MSC official once remarked. "In fact, much of our related technical work right down to film developing will be done by local firms."[40] And this reliance, this dependence upon the surrounding community, opens another chapter of the MSC story, that is, how the space center utilized local schools and industry and, in so doing, how it brought about changes in each that would significantly affect Houston's way of life.

In the area of public education, to begin with, the center's needs were critical and far-reaching. It depended on the public schools for the nation's future space scientists and technicians. It relied on them to give tomorrow's electorate a broader, basic scientific education so that, in later years, the nation's rich heritage of popular government and democratic exploration of space might indeed prevail. Accordingly, the space center from the outset had a close working relationship with Houston's schools, implementing their regular curricula with spacemobile lectures and planned school exhibits. The center also inaugurated a teacher-trainer program in which schoolteachers, once each week, could receive at MSC laboratories on-the-job training in space sciences and computer mathematics. This program in turn encouraged more enlightened instruction in the classrooms them-

[39] *MSC Constructing Permanent Facilities at Clear Lake* (NASA Fact Sheet #60), 1–4.
[40] Paul E. Purser, *Questions and Answers*, 2.

selves, not only in the regular courses of biology, chemistry, and physics, but also in special mathematics and exploratory science courses offered to gifted pupils each summer.[41]

On the university level, the center's needs—and therefore its influences—were far greater. It needed the universities to extend the education of NASA's future scientists, to do creative research in support of the nation's space objectives, and to instruct MSC personnel on the latest advances in such fields as thermodynamics and biochemistry, higher mathematics and astronomy. These needs impelled MSC, during its first summer in Houston, to work out a cooperating program with Rice University, the University of Houston, the Baylor University College of Medicine, and Texas A and M—a program that might one day make these institutions the principal research and creative source for MSC's space projects.

The program itself, begun in the fall of 1962, took several forms. One was a prompt exchange of brainpower, a give and take of ideas, with MSC scientists lecturing in university classrooms and university professors in MSC laboratories. Another was a special graduate training course which Rice, the University of Houston, and Texas A and M offered to some 125 MSC technical personnel.[42] Still another was the start of a long-range MSC plan to give these institutions several thousand dollars for graduate student fellowships.[43]

The most vital facet of the program, though, was in the area of co-operative research. Here the Manned Spacecraft Center merely extended a practice NASA had already be-

[41] Horton to S. B. O., Houston, interview, July 22, 1963; John W. McFarland, Superintendent of the Houston Independent School District, to S. B. O., Houston, interview, August 2, 1963.

[42] Paul E. Purser, Special Assistant to the Director, Manned Spacecraft Center, to S. B. O., Houston, interview, July 22, 1963; Yeater, *The NASA Manned Spacecraft Center and Its Programs*, 5–6; *Houston Magazine*, March, 1963, p. 28.

[43] "First Year: Space-Age Impact on Houston," *Houston Magazine*, September, 1962, p. 33; Lang, Purchase Request for the Moon, 10.

gun, that of giving the universities and other science facilities grants or contracts for special research.[44] The space center gave the Baylor University College of Medicine, for example, a grant to develop a means of monitoring astronauts' brain waves during flights. The college started experiments at once on two hundred pilots—some potential astronauts—at the Methodist Hospital's new space-neurobiology laboratory. Elsewhere in the Texas Medical Center, of which the Baylor college was a part, other research-training-treatment centers had already begun work with the space center on such vital projects as environmental control, life-systems research, and space medicine.[45]

At the same time, the Manned Spacecraft Center started additional research projects at the universities over the area. It gave Rice several new NASA grants and implemented old ones, bringing the university's total to seventeen grants amounting to $300,000 a year for research in chemistry and physics and in electrical, chemical, and mechanical engineering.[46] The center next brought the University of Houston into the program through a $71,250 grant to two of its chemistry professors to develop miniature instruments which would measure the chemical composition of the moon and other celestial bodies for evidence of life.[47] Then MSC reached beyond Houston to Texas A and M University, eighty miles to the northwest near Bryan, whose Nuclear Science Center owned the only nuclear reactor associated

[44] Lang, Purchase Request for the Moon, 10.

[45] Ben Gillespie, Chief of Industrial Communications Branch, Manned Spacecraft Center, to S. B. O., Houston, interview, July 22, 1963; *Houston Magazine*, September, 1962, p. 33, June, 1963, p. 32. The Aeromedical Division of the Air Force Systems Command at Brooks Air Force Base, San Antonio, was also developing space medicines and was, in addition, studying the effect of space travel on human beings. Purser to S. B. O., Houston, interview, July 22, 1963.

[46] Kenneth S. Pitzer, president of Rice University, to James M. Grimwood, January 4, 1963 (photostatic copy of letter in possession of the author); *Houston Magazine*, July, 1962, p. 24.

[47] *Ibid.*, September, 1962, p. 34, October, 1962, p. 27.

with a southwestern college. MSC gave a team of scientists there an $84,860 grant to determine the feasibility of learning the elemental composition of the moon's surface, then awarded A and M engineers $52,100 to study how low-level turbulent winds affected large rockets on their launching pads.[48]

As the space team had hoped, these grants and the promise of more to follow literally started all three schools on a campaign for space science excellence. Texas A and M promptly added a space technology division to its Texas Engineering Experiment Station, then revised its current curriculum to include several space-related courses.[49] MSC likewise spurred the University of Houston along new directions of growth. Assisted by advisers from the space center and local industry, the administration there undertook a broad internal study of the university to discover how best it could adjust itself to Space Age requirements. This led to a new interdisciplinary program—an enriched curriculum in all fields of study to attract "the highly qualified high school graduate"—and to such an upgrading of its graduate school that the Texas Commission on Higher Education at last approved University of Houston Ph.D. programs in chemical and electrical engineering.[50] By the time the university got state support in 1963, it was well on its way toward becoming a truly respectable academic institution.

Neither Texas A and M nor the University of Houston, however, could match the growth of Rice University, already one of the top twenty prestige institutions in the nation and one of the chief factors in NASA's move to Houston. Striving to make itself "a symbol of Space Age Science," Rice

[48] *Ibid.*, July, 1962, p. 24, September, 1962, p. 34.
[49] *Ibid.*, June, 1963, p. 32.
[50] Philip G. Hoffman, president of the University of Houston, to James M. Grimwood, January 4, 1963 (photostatic copy of letter in possession of the author).

185

launched a "three to seven year" plan in 1962 to improve and expand engineering facilities, to accelerate research projects both old and new, to add to the graduate faculty some fifty first-rate scholars in various fields of research, and, without sacrificing the university's reputation for quality, to increase graduate school capacity from 350 to 800.[51] Rice's greatest advance, though, came in the academic year 1963–64 when it established a department of space science, the first university in the nation to do so. This department came about largely through the efforts of Rice president Kenneth S. Pitzer, who as a chemist and former research director of the Atomic Energy Commission had powerful convictions about the role of the university in the nation's scientific progress. In the department's initial semester it offered qualified students basic courses in several space fields that ranged from the dynamic characteristics of the interplanetary medium to the Van Allen radiation belts that circle the earth. The department also worked closely with the Manned Spacecraft Center, bringing in several of its experts to lecture on the most recent advances in spacecraft engineering. Meanwhile, Rice's other technical and mathematics departments, working with three huge computers and one of the fastest electronic "brains" in the world, with two Van de Graff atom smashers and vast lab facilities, had expanded their own programs to cover many of the fringe areas of space technology. Even with that, Rice had come nowhere near realizing its full potential.[52] With continuing co-operation from the Manned Spacecraft Center, the university could look ahead toward brilliant new dimensions in education and scholarship.

As the space center had utilized Houston's education and

[51] "First Year: Space-Age Impact on Houston," *Houston Magazine*, September, 1962, p. 30.

[52] Pitzer to Grimwood, January 4, 1963; *Houston Magazine*, February, 1963, p. 30.

research facilities, so it likewise drew heavily on the city's economy for those things which it could not itself provide. As a result, by August, 1963, the center was spending over $1 million a month in contracts with some five hundred local firms for services of all kinds—for supplies and equipment parts (such as typewriters, instruments, valves), for thermochemicals, electronics and computer research, for communications, utilities, and skilled and unskilled labor. At that date, MSC had already spent $5,342,111 in Houston, which was more than two-thirds of the sum it had spent in Texas at large—$8,202,545. In addition, the center had committed over $80 million more in current or active contracts with firms in the Houston area, and with some in San Antonio, Dallas, Fort Worth, and El Paso. In terms of MSC's national expenditures—$11,737,977 already spent and over $1.1 billion more allotted in active contracts—Texas businessmen had pocketed some 61 per cent of completed contract dollars and would get about 7 per cent of active contract dollars, with Houston-area concerns accounting for most of Texas' percentages.[53] Furthermore, the center had spent most of the $150 million authorized for the permanent facilities at Clear Lake, and "the majority of these expenditures" had gone to Houston enterprises for materials and labor.[54]

The total percentages given above, though, did not include the vast sums of money pouring into the Houston economy in the form of subcontracts, that is, contracts which the firms doing business with MSC let to other industrial organizations for special work. Over 70 per cent of MSC's active "prime" contracts was spent in this manner, and a large portion of this percentage went to Houston businesses. For example, of the forty-four subcontracts awarded by Leavell,

[53] Gillespie to S. B. O., Houston, interview, July 22, 1963.
[54] Lang, Purchase Request for the Moon, 6.

Morrison-Knudsen and Hardeman, which did $19.2 million worth of preliminary construction at Clear Lake, thirty-three went to enterprises in the Houston area. Likewise, Ets-Hokin and Galvan, Inc., whose construction contracts with MSC totaled $8.5 million, gave twenty-nine of its thirty-two subcontracts to Houston firms. Other industrial and aerospace outfits from outside Houston which had MSC contracts—North American Aviation, Philco, and Grumman Aircraft, to name a few—no doubt let similar percentages of subcontracts to local businesses, so that the total number of space dollars spent in the Houston area by August, 1963, must have been in the millions of dollars. And this did not count the salaries to MSC employees, which amounted to $2.3 million a month and which rose to $3.2 million by April, 1964, when the number of MSC personnel leveled off at about five thousand. Since at least half of these came from outside Houston, they bought an estimated $37 million worth of new homes. And what they all spent on new automobiles, supplies, services, furniture, clothing, and everything else took most of their yearly income—about $38.4 million—into the Houston economy.[55]

What did all these expenditures mean? Did they portend a veritable economic explosion in Houston? The Chamber of Commerce there certainly believed so; it had already forecast that the arrival of the Manned Spacecraft Center would start an economic boom similar to that caused by the opening of the ship channel over fifty years earlier, that it would divert Houston's industrial growth from an almost total reliance on the petrochemical industry onto new vectors of progress in aerospace and electronics activity. By August, 1963, the Chamber of Commerce could point to certain facts

[55] *Ibid.*, 8–9; Houston *Chronicle*, July 27, 1963; Yeater, *The NASA Manned Spacecraft Center and Its Programs*, 4. See also Swenson, "The Fertile Crescent," *Southwestern Historical Quarterly*, LXXI, 388–89.

and figures, trends and innovations, that proved its earlier predictions more than right.

To begin with, over one hundred aerospace firms with major MSC contracts had opened district or liaison offices in Houston, and the number was increasing virtually every week.[56] One of the first to do so had been North American Aviation which had organized district offices for two of its space-related divisions—Autonetics and Rocketdyne—in 1962. This move proved to be "a vote of confidence in Houston's expanding role in the scientific and missile fields,"[57] for in the following months all of MSC's prime contractors established local offices there: McDonnell Aircraft, Grumman Aircraft, Philco (a subdivision of Ford Motor Co.), and Lockheed Aircraft Corporation. Lockheed, in addition, "to meet any Space Age opportunities that may occur," bought 550 acres of land near MSC's Clear Lake site for possible construction of lab and testing facilities.[58] After that, the number of new space-related enterprises moving into the city rose sharply. Boeing Aircraft and General Electric Company came in; so did International Business Machines, Brown Engineering, United Aircraft, and a score of computer and electronics firms. In terms of manpower, these outfits brought with them literally hundreds of scientists and engineers; Philco's new office alone accounted for 450, General Electric for 100, with plans to add 250 more in 1964.[59]

This influx of industrial and scientific firms co-operating with MSC had truly phenomenal results. For one thing, as the Texas Employment Commission happily discovered, it opened in Houston "almost unlimited opportunities in the

56 Houston Chamber of Commerce, *Space Industry Firms & Representatives Presently Located in Houston, Texas, May 3, 1963*; Gillespie to S. B. O., Houston, interview, July 22, 1963.

57 *Houston Magazine*, November, 1962, p. 24.

58 *Ibid.*, February, 1963, p. 29.

59 *Ibid.*, June, 1963, pp. 32–34; Robert H. Brewer, Houston Chamber of Commerce, to S. B. O., Houston, Interview, August 2, 1963.

field of space technology."[60] It created new businesses, expanded old ones, increased the demand for investment and skilled personnel, and inspired diversification in the oil industry. In 1962 alone, ten computer companies transferred to Houston to compete for MSC contracts or to work with the new aerospace firms and thus "get some of the fall-out from the main effort."[61] At the same time Houston oil outfits like Reed Roller Bit, Hughes Tool, Mission Manufacturing, Cameron Iron Works, and Schlumberger—all heretofore exclusively oil-field enterprises—promptly organized aerospace or electronics subsidiaries and started competing as well.[62] So did Houston-based Brown and Root, Ruska Instrument Corporation, and Gulf Interstate Engineering Consultants.[63] Such growth, such diversification and expansion, in turn stimulated virtually every other form of business activity. Manufacturing sales rose higher and faster than ever before.[64] Banking activity increased markedly over 1961.[65] And flights at the Houston International Airport went up 7 per cent as over three hundred businessmen a month flew in to visit the Manned Spacecraft Center and to discuss with the Chamber of Commerce the advantages of

[60] Texas Employment Commission, *Manpower Patterns Through 1966 . . . in the Eight-County Houston-Gulf Coast Area*, 4.

[61] William A. Parker, Remarks on the Impact of the Space Age: Presented to the Houston Financial Institute Executives, February 26, 1963 (typescript, Manned Spacecraft Center, Houston) ; Brewer to S. B. O., Houston, interview, August 2, 1963.

[62] Brewer to S. B. O.; John Moody, *Moody's Industrial Manual*, 2043.

[63] *Houston Magazine*, May, 1962, p. 24; Brewer to S. B. O., Houston, interview, August 2, 1963.

[64] Houston Chamber of Commerce, *Growth and Development of Houston and Harris County: A Statistical Summary*, 1, 3, 6–7; Houston Chamber of Commerce, *Monthly Statistical Summary, June, 1963*, p. 6.

[65] According to Lloyd Thomas, Supervising Examiner for the Eleventh Federal Reserve District, who in July, 1963, ran a survey of Texas banking activities, the Manned Spacecraft Center at Houston was "sparking an economic explosion" not only in its immediate area, but over the state as well. The number of banks in Texas had leaped to an unprecedented 1,030—more than any other state. In the fiscal year 1962–63 total deposits in Texas banks rose $589 million and total bank assets $959 million, a substantial increase over 1961–62. United Press International in Houston *Chronicle*, July 29, 1963.

moving to Houston.[66] Everywhere, across the city, over the Bay area, there were growing signs of the beginnings of an economic revolution.

Nowhere were these signs more visible than at Clear Lake. There, in a half-moon of prairie about the permanent space center, construction teams were building an extraordinary new city. Just south of the center and east of it along the lake, countless new homes, almost surrealistic in design, were already complete and open for sale. Huge apartment buildings, sky-reaching offices and hotels, and hundreds of additional homes were going up there as well,[67] while adjacent to the MSC site and beyond, to the west and northwest, Humble Oil and Refining Company and Del Webb, Inc., were building a fantastic community complex called Clear Lake City. This development, sprawling over 15,000 acres, costing from $200 to $375 million, involved a novel "recreation city" concept in community living, with a downtown area of twenty-seven or more skyscrapers, a vortex of offices and shops, schools and labs, with a vast network of medical centers, parks, cultural facilities, sports coliseums, and civic centers, and finally with an enormous residential area whose ultramodern homes would epitomize the impact of the Space Age on American architecture.[68] This building boom, precipitated by the arrival of the Manned Spacecraft Center, accelerated by prospects of a mass influx into Houston of industry, scientists, and wealth-seeking entrepreneurs, portended incredible things. The University of Houston Bu-

[66] Lang, Purchase Request for the Moon, 7.

[67] The firms engaged in building these additional homes, apartments, and offices were Richmond Realty Co., constructing a $300,000 professional building near the space center; Nassau Bay Development Associates (a combination of Houston business outfits), building on a 570-acre site south of the space center a complex of 400 apartments, 15 office buildings, 1,000 homes, and several stores; and Astral Towers Limited, constructing twin tower apartment buildings not far from the space center along Farm Road 528. *Houston Magazine*, September, 1962, pp. 24–25.

[68] *Ibid.*, March, 1963, pp. 24–26; Houston *Chronicle*, August 29, 1962.

reau of Business Research predicted that within two decades the Clear Lake Developments, taken collectively, would create technical and research jobs for 70,000 people, would attract some 207,200 new residents, and would add to the area's economy $406 million in personal income, $182 million in bank deposits, $140 million in annual property taxes, and $245 million in increased retail sales.[69] The Texas National Bank, which sponsored an economic survey called "The Houston Orbit," went even further. Within fifty years, it believed, the Bay-Channel area around the Manned Spacecraft Center would have a million people in it; at the same time, Greater Houston would swell to an enormous 7.8 million people, whose income and business and technical activities would involve billions of dollars.[70]

There were other predictions, too, predictions that Houston would one day become the nation's leading scientific-industrial community. Some even went beyond that as men's imaginations soared, and their minds peered far into the future. To Houstonians at large, there seemed virtually no end to the possibilities created by the Manned Spacecraft Center and by the innovations which it inspired in community building, related industry, and supporting research. Looking ahead with irrevocable expectation, a booming Texas metropolis, excited beyond memory, stimulated as it had never been before, moved inexorably across the bridge of mid-century into the limitless frontiers of a new time— a time when man would leave the planet of his birth and reach out, beyond, into the distant splendor of the stars themselves.

[69] *Houston Magazine*, March, 1963, p. 26.
[70] *Ibid.*, June, 1962, p. 24.

General Bibliography

MANUSCRIPTS

Baker, J. H. Diary. Archives Collection of the University of Texas Library, Austin.

Ballinger, William Pitt. Diaries, 1854 to 1886. Typescript. Archives Collection of the University of Texas Library, Austin.

Brown, Frank. "Annals of Travis County and the City of Austin from the Earliest Times to the Close of 1875." Typescript. Archives Division of the Texas State Library, Austin.

Burleson, Ed. Papers. Archives Collection of the University of Texas Library, Austin.

Emme, Eugene M. Administrator's Progress Report for March, 1963. Typescript. Photostatic copy in possession of the author.

Felgar, Robert Pattison. "Texas in the War for Southern Independence, 1861–1865." Ph.D. dissertation, University of Texas, 1935.

Ford, John S. Letter Books. 3 vols., typescript. Archives Division of the Texas State Library, Austin.

———. Memoirs. 7 vols., typescript. Archives Collection of the University of Texas Library, Austin.

Goodlet, Margaret N. "The Enforcement of the Confederate Conscription Acts in the Trans-Mississippi Department." Master's thesis, University of Texas, 1914.

Hayden, Carl. Biographical Information Sheet sent to Harriet Smithers. Archives Division of the Texas State Library, Austin.

Hébert, Paul Octave. Service Record. Confederate Records of the U.S. War Department, National Archives, Washington, D.C.

Hoffman, Philip G. Letter to James M. Grimwood, January 4, 1963. Photostatic copy in possession of the author.

Lang, Dave W. Purchase Request for the Moon. Typescript. Photostatic copy in possession of the author.

Lubbock, Francis R. Governor's Letters in Executive Correspondence. Archives Division of the Texas State Library, Austin.

Megee, Jonnie M. "The Confederate Impressment Acts of the Trans-Mississippi States." Master's thesis, University of Texas, 1915.

Murrah, Pendleton. Letter Books. 3 vols. Archives Division of the Texas State Library, Austin.

Neighbours, Kenneth Franklin. "Robert S. Neighbors in Texas, 1836–1859: A Quarter Century of Frontier Problems." Ph.D. dissertation, University of Texas, 1955.

Nichols, James L. "Confederate Quartermaster Operations in the Trans-Mississippi Department." Master's thesis, University of Texas, 1947.

Parker, William A. Remarks on the Impact of the Space Age: Presented to the Houston Financial Institute Executives, February 26, 1963. Typescript. NASA's Manned Spacecraft Center, Houston, Texas.

Pitzer, Kenneth S. Letter to James M. Grimwood, January 4, 1963. Photostatic copy in possession of the author.

Roberts, O. M. Papers. Archives Collection of the University of Texas Library, Austin.

Texas (Confederate State). Senate Journal, 9th Leg., 1st called sess., February 2 to March 7, 1863. Archives Division of the Texas State Library, Austin.

———. Senate Journal, 10th Leg., 1st called sess., May 9 to May 28, 1864. Archives Division of the Texas State Library, Austin.

———. Senate Journal, 10th Leg., 2d called sess., October 17 to November 14, 1864. Archives Division of the Texas State Library, Austin.

Texas (Republic). Army Papers, 1840–1845. Archives Division of the Texas State Library, Austin.

Texas (State and Confederate State). Governors' Letters, 1846–1865. Archives Division of the Texas State Library, Austin.

U.S. War Department. Records Group No. 94. National Archives, Washington, D.C.

Newspapers and News Magazines

Chronicle (Houston), 1961–63.
Congressional Globe (Washington, D.C.), 1846–52.
Countryman (Bellville), 1861.
Delta (New Orleans), 1848.
Democrat (Belton), 1861.
Democratic Telegraph and Texas Register (Columbia and Houston), 1845, 1848, 1850.
Enterprise (Beaumont), 1901.
Express (San Antonio), 1890.
Herald (Dallas), 1861–62, 1961.
Herald (San Antonio), 1861.
Houston Magazine, 1961–62.
Morning News (Dallas), 1961–62.
Niles National Register (Baltimore), 1847.
Northern Standard (Clarksville), 1843.
Picayune (New Orleans), 1847.
Pioneer (San Jose, Calif.), 1901.
Post (Houston), 1961–63.
State Gazette (Austin), 1857, 1860.
Texas Almanac–Extra (Austin), 1862–63.
Texas Democrat (Austin), 1846–49.
Texas State Gazette (Austin), 1860–61, 1865.
Times (Wichita Falls), 1961.
Tri-Weekly News (Galveston), 1865.
Tri-Weekly Telegraph (Houston), 1860, 1862–63.

Books

Anderson, John Q. *A Texas Surgeon in the C.S.A.* Tuscaloosa, Alabama, Confederate Publishing Co., 1957.

Barron, Samuel B. *The Lone Star Defenders: A Chronicle of the Third Texas Cavalry, Ross' Brigade.* New York and Washington, Neale Publishing Co., 1908.

Barry, James Buckner. *A Texas Ranger and Frontiersman: The Days of Buck Barry in Texas, 1845–1906.* Edited by James K. Greer. Dallas, Southwest Press, 1932.

Benjamin, Gilbert C. *The Germans in Texas.* New York, D. Appleton & Co., 1907.

Biggers, Don H. *German Pioneers in Texas.* Fredericksburg, Texas, Fredericksburg Publishing Co., 1925.

Binkley, William C. *The Expansionist Movement in Texas, 1836–1850.* Berkeley, University of California Press, 1925.

Blessington, Joseph. *The Campaigns of Walker's Texas Division.* New York, Lang, Little & Co., 1875.

Boatright, Mody C. *Folklore of the Oil Industry.* Dallas, Southern Methodist University Press, 1963.

Bosque, Edward. *Memoirs.* San Francisco, n.p., 1904.

Brackett, Albert G. *General Lane's Brigade in Central Mexico.* Cincinnati, H. W. Derby & Co., 1854.

———. *History of the United States Cavalry, from the Formation of the Federal Government to the 1st of June, 1863.* New York, Harper & Brothers, 1865.

Brown, John Henry. *History of Texas from 1685 to 1892.* 2 vols. St. Louis, L. E. Daniell, 1893.

Clark, James A., and Michel T. Halbouty. *Spindletop.* New York, Random House, 1952.

Cooke, John Esten. *Wearing of the Gray: Being Personal Portraits, Scenes and Adventures of the War.* New York, E. B. Treat & Co., 1867.

Dimitry, John. "Louisiana," in Volume X of *Confederate Military History.* Edited by Clement A. Evans. 12 vols. Atlanta, Confederate Publishing Co., 1899.

Dyer, John P. *The Gallant Hood.* Indianapolis and New York, Bobbs-Merrill Co., 1950.

Edwards, John N. *Shelby and His Men: Or, the War in the West.* Cincinnati, Miami Printing & Publishing Co., 1867.

Fitzhugh, Lester N., comp. *Texas Batteries, Battalions, Regiments, Commanders and Field Officers Confederate States Army, 1861–1865.* Midlothian, Texas, Mirror Press, 1959.

Fletcher, William A. *Rebel Private Front and Rear.* Edited by Bell I. Wiley. Austin, University of Texas Press, 1954.

Ford, John S. *Rip Ford's Texas.* Edited by Stephen B. Oates. Austin, University of Texas Press, 1963.

Fornell, Earl W. *The Galveston Era: The Texas Crescent on the Eve of Secession.* Austin, University of Texas Press, 1961.

Franklin, Robert M. *The Battle of Galveston, January 1st, 1863.* Galveston, Galveston News, 1911.

Fremantle, Arthur James Lyon. *The Fremantle Diary.* Edited by Walter Lord. Boston, Little, Brown, 1954.

Friend, Llerena B. *Sam Houston, the Great Designer.* Austin, University of Texas Press, 1954.

George, Isaac. *Heroes and Incidents of the Mexican War.* Greensburg, Pennsylvania, Review Publishing Co., 1903.

[Giddings, Luther.] *Sketches of the Campaign in Northern Mexico in Eighteen Hundred Forty-Six and Seven by an Officer of the First Ohio Volunteers.* New York, G. P. Putnam & Co., 1853.

Giles, L. B. *Terry's Texas Rangers.* Austin, Von Boeckmann-Jones, 1911.

Gray, Alonzo. *Cavalry Tactics as Illustrated by the War of the Rebellion.* Fort Leavenworth, U.S. Cavalry Association, 1910.

The Gray Jackets; and How They Lived, Fought, and Died, For Dixie, With Incidents and Sketches of Life in the Confederacy. Richmond, 1867.

Greer, James Kimmons. *Colonel Jack Hayes: Texas Frontier Leader and California Builder.* New York, E. P. Dutton, 1952.

Gregg, Josiah. *Commerce of the Prairies: The Journal of a Santa Fe Trader.* 2 vols. Philadelphia, J. W. Moore, 1855.

Griffith, Alison E. *The Genesis of the National Aeronautics and Space Act of 1958.* Washington, Public Affairs Press, 1962.

Hall, Martin Hardwick. *Sibley's New Mexico Campaign.* Austin, University of Texas Press, 1960.

Hay, T. R. *Hood's Tennessee Campaign.* New York, W. Neale Co., 1929.

Heartsill, William W. *Fourteen Hundred and Ninety-One Days in the Confederate Army: or, Camp Life, Day by Day, of the W. P. Lane Rangers from April 19, 1861 to May 20, 1865.* Facsimile reprint of 1876 edition. Edited by Bell I. Wiley. Jackson, Tennessee, McCowat-Mercer Press, 1954.

Hitchcock, Ethan A. *Fifty Years in Camp and Field.* Edited by W. A. Croffut. New York, G. P. Putnam & Sons, 1909.

Holmes, Jay. *America on the Moon: the Enterprise of the 60's.* Philadelphia, Lippincott, 1962.

Holmes, Sarah Kate (Stone). *Brokenburn: The Journal of Kate Stone, 1861–1868.* Edited by John Q. Anderson. Baton Rouge, Louisiana State University Press, 1955.

Hood, J. B. *Advance and Retreat: Personal Experiences in the United States and Confederate Armies.* New Orleans, Published for the Hood Orphan Memorial Fund, 1880.

Horgan, Paul. *Great River: The Rio Grande in North American History.* 2 vols. New York, Holt, Rinehart & Winston, 1954.

House, Boyce. *Oil Boom.* Caxton, Idaho, Caxton Printers, 1941.

Houston, Samuel. *The Writings of Sam Houston.* Edited by Amelia W. Williams and Eugene C. Barker. 8 vols. Austin, University of Texas Press, 1938–43.

Houston Chamber of Commerce. *Growth and Development of Houston and Harris County: A Statistical Summary.* Houston, 1963.

———. *Monthly Statistical Summary, June, 1963.* Houston, 1963.

———. *Space Industry Firms & Representatives Presently Located in Houston, Texas, May 3, 1963.* Houston, 1963.

Hughes, W. J. *Rebellious Ranger: Rip Ford and the Old Southwest.* Norman, University of Oklahoma Press, 1964.

James, Marquis. *The Raven: A Biography of Sam Houston.* New York, Blue Ribbon Books, 1929.

Jastrow, Robert, ed. *The Exploration of Space.* New York, Macmillan Co., 1960.

Jeffries, C. C. *Terry's Rangers.* New York, Vantage Press, 1961.

Johnson, Allen, and Dumas Malone, eds. *Dictionary of American Biography.* 20 vols. New York, Charles Scribner's Sons, 1928–36.

Johnson, Frank W. *A History of Texas and Texans.* Edited by Eugene C. Barker. 5 vols. Chicago and New York, American Historical Society, 1914.

Johnson, Robert V., and Clarence C. Buel, eds. *Battles and Leaders of the Civil War.* Facsimile reprint of 1887–88 edition. 4 vols. New York, Thomas Yoseloff, 1956.

Kenly, John R. *Memoirs of a Maryland Volunteer, War with Mexico, in the Years 1846-7-8.* Philadelphia, J. B. Lippincott, 1873.

Knowles, Ruth Sheldon. *The Greatest Gamblers: The Epic of American Oil Exploration.* New York, McGraw-Hill, 1959.

Lamar, Mirabeau Bounaparte. *The Papers of Mirabeau Bounaparte Lamar.* Edited by C. A. Gulick, Jr., and others. 6 vols. Austin, Von Boeckmann-Jones, 1921–27.

Ley, Willy. *Rockets, Missiles, and Space Travel.* New York, Viking Press, 1961.

Lubbock, Francis R. *Six Decades in Texas.* Austin, Ben C. Jones & Co., 1900.

McKee, James Cooper. *Narrative of the Surrender of a Command of U.S. Forces at Fort Fillmore, New Mexico, in July, A.D., 1861, with Related Reports by John R. Baylor, C.S.A., and Others.* Houston, Stagecoach Press, 1960.

Malloy, William M., comp. *Treaties, Conventions, International Acts, Protocols, and Agreements Between the United States and Other Powers, 1776–1909.* 2 vols. Washington, D.C., Government Printing Office, 1910.

Melish, John. *A Geographical Description of the World, Intended as an Accompaniment to the Map of the World on Mercator's Projection.* Philadelphia, John Melish & Samuel Harrison, 1818.

Moody, John. *Moody's Industrial Manual.* New York, Moody's Investors Service, 1963.

Nichols, James L. *The Confederate Quartermaster in the Trans-Mississippi.* Austin, University of Texas Press, 1964.

Noel, Theo. *A Campaign from Santa Fe to the Mississippi: Being a History of the Old Sibley Brigade.* Reprint of 1865 edition. Edited by Martin Hardwick Hall and Edwin Adams Davis. Houston, Stagecoach Press, 1961.

North, Thomas. *Five Years in Texas: Or, What You Did Not Hear during the War from January 1861 to January 1866.* Cincinnati, Elm Street Printing Co., 1871.

Oates, Stephen B. *Confederate Cavalry West of the River.* Austin, University of Texas Press, 1961.

Oliva, Leo E. *Soldiers on the Santa Fe Trail.* Norman, University of Oklahoma Press, 1967.

Oswandel, J. J. *Notes on the Mexican War, 1846–47–48.* Philadelphia, n.p., 1885.

Parks, Joseph H. *General Edmund Kirby Smith, C.S.A.* Baton Rouge, Louisiana State University Press, 1954.

Reid, S. C., Jr. *The Scouting Expeditions of McCulloch's Texas Rangers.* Philadelphia, G. B. Zieber & Co., 1847.

Richardson, T. C. *East Texas: Its History and Its Makers.* 4 vols. New York, Lewis Historical Publishing Co., 1881.

Rister, Carl Coke. *Oil! Titan of the Southwest.* Norman, University of Oklahoma Press, 1949.

Roberts, Oran M. "Texas," in Volume XI of *Confederate Military History.* Edited by Clement A. Evans. 12 vols. Atlanta, Confederate Publishing Co., 1899.

Rose, Victor M. *Ross' Texas Brigade.* Louisville, Courier-Journal Job Printing Co., 1881.

199

Sage, Rufus B. *Scenes in the Rocky Mountains, and the Grand Prairies.* Philadelphia, Carey & Hart, 1846.

Sansom, John W. *Battle of Nueces River in Kinney County, Texas, August 10th, 1862.* San Antonio, n.p., 1905.

Singletary, Otis A. *The Mexican War.* Chicago, University of Chicago Press, 1960.

Smith, Justin H. *The War with Mexico.* 2 vols. New York, Macmillan Co., 1919.

Swenson, Loyd S., Jr., James M. Grimwood, and Charles C. Alexander. *This New Ocean: A History of Project Mercury.* Washington, D.C., National Aeronautics & Space Administration, 1966.

Taylor, Richard. *Destruction and Reconstruction: Personal Experiences in the Late War.* New York, D. Appleton & Co., 1879.

Texas Adjutant General. *Report, November, 1861.* Austin, 1961.

Texas Employment Commission. *Manpower Patterns Through 1966 . . . in the Eight-County Houston-Gulf Coast Area.* Austin, 1962.

Texas Governor, March 16–November 7, 1861 (Edward Clark). *Governor's Message: Executive Office, Austin, March 29, 1861.* [Austin, John Marshall & Co., 1861.]

———. *Governor's Message to the Senators and Representatives of the Ninth Legislature of the State of Texas, November 1, 1861.* Austin, John Marshall & Co., 1861.

U.S. Congress, *House Executive Documents.* 29th Cong., 2d sess., No. 4. Washington, D.C., Richie & Heiss, 1846. Serial 497.

———. *House Executive Documents.* 30th Cong., 1st sess., No. 60. Washington, D.C., Wendell & Van Benthuysen, 1848. Serial 520.

———. *House Executive Documents.* 30th Cong., 2d sess., No. 1. Washington, D.C., Wendell & Van Benthuysen, 1848. Serial 537.

———. *Senate Executive Documents.* 30th Cong., 1st sess., No. 1. Washington, D.C., Wendell & Van Benthuysen, 1847. Serial 503.

———. *Statutes at Large, 1847.* Vol. IX.

U.S. War Department. *Memorandum Relative to the General Officers . . . of the Confederate States, 1861–1865.* Washington, D.C., Government Printing Office, 1905.

———. *Official Records of the Union and Confederate Navies in the War of the Rebellion.* 31 vols. Washington, D.C., Government Printing Office, 1894–1927.

———. *The War of the Rebellion: A Compilation of the Official Records of the Union and Confederate Armies.* 70 vols. in 128. Washington, D.C., Government Printing Office, 1880–1901.

Vandiver, Frank E. *Ploughshares into Swords: Josiah Gorgas and Confederate Ordnance*. Austin, University of Texas Press, 1952.

Warner, C. A. *Texas Oil and Gas Since 1543*. Houston, Gulf Publishing Co., 1939.

Webb, Walter Prescott. *The Texas Rangers: A Century of Frontier Defense*. Boston, Houghton Mifflin, 1935.

———, and H. Bailey Carroll, eds. *Handbook of Texas*. 2 vols. Austin, Texas State Historical Association, 1952.

Williams, R. H. *With the Border Ruffians: Memoirs of the Far West, 1852–1868*. London, E. P. Dutton & Co., 1907.

Winkler, E. W., ed. *Journal of the Secession Convention of Texas, 1861*. Austin, Austin Printing Co., 1912.

Wooten, Dudley G., ed. *A Comprehensive History of Texas*. 2 vols. Dallas, W. G. Scarff, 1898.

W.P.A. Federal Writers' Project. *Beaumont: A Guide to the City and Its Environs*. Houston, n.d.

Yoakum, Henderson. *History of Texas from Its First Settlement in 1685 to Its Annexation to the United States in 1846*. 2 vols. New York, J. S. Redfield, 1855.

Young, Hugh H. *Hugh Young: A Surgeon's Autobiography*. New York, Harcourt, Brace & Co., 1940.

ARTICLES

Acheson, Sam, and Julie Ann Hudson, eds. "George Washington Diamond's Account of the Great Hanging at Gainsville, 1862," *Southwestern Historical Quarterly*, LXVI (January, 1963).

Baker, William Mumford. "A Pivotal Point," *Lippincott's Magazine*, XXVI (November, 1880).

Barr, Alwyn. "Sabine Pass, September, 1863," *Texas Military History*, II (February, 1962).

———. "Texas Coastal Defense, 1862–1865," *Southwestern Historical Quarterly*, LXV (July, 1961).

Bender, A. B. "Opening Routes Across West Texas," *Southwestern Historical Quarterly*, XXXVII (October, 1933).

Blackburn, J. K. P. "Reminiscences of the Terry Rangers," *Southwestern Historical Quarterly*, XXII (July and October, 1918).

Carroll, H. Bailey. "Steward A. Miller and the Snively Expedition," *Southwestern Historical Quarterly*, LIV (January, 1951).

Connelley, William E., ed. "A Journal of the Santa Fe Trail," *Mississippi Valley Historical Review*, XII (September, 1905).

Cumberland, Charles C. "The Confederate Loss and Recapture of Galveston, 1862–1863," *Southwestern Historical Quarterly*, LI (October, 1947).

DeGoyler, E. "Anthony F. Lucas at Spindletop," *Southwest Review*, XXXI (Fall, 1945).

Elliott, Claude. "Union Sentiment in Texas, 1861–1865," *Southwestern Historical Quarterly*, L (April, 1947).

Ewing, Floyd F., Jr. "Origins of Unionist Sentiment on the West Texas Frontier," *West Texas Historical Association Year Book*, XXXII (October, 1956).

———. "Unionist Sentiment on the Northwest Texas Frontier," *West Texas Historical Association Year Book*, XXXIII (October, 1957).

Hill, R. T. "The Beaumont Oil Field, With Notes on Other Oil Fields of the Texas Region," *Journal of the Franklin Institute*, August–October, 1902.

Muir, Andrew Forest. "Dick Dowling and the Battle of Sabine Pass," *Civil War History*, IV (December, 1958).

Neighbors, Robert S. "The Report of the Expedition of Major Robert S. Neighbors to El Paso in 1849" (ed. Kenneth F. Neighbours), *Southwestern Historical Quarterly*, LX (April, 1957).

Neighbours, Kenneth F. "The Expedition of Major Robert S. Neighbors to El Paso in 1849," *Southwestern Historical Quarterly*, LVIII (July, 1954).

Oates, Stephen B. "Confederate Cavalrymen of the Trans-Mississippi," *Civil War History*, VII (March, 1961).

———. "John S. 'Rip' Ford: Prudent Cavalryman, C.S.A.," *Southwestern Historical Quarterly*, LXIV (January, 1961).

———. "Supply for Confederate Cavalry in the Trans-Mississippi," *Military Affairs*, XXV (Summer, 1961).

———, ed. "Hugh F. Young's Account of the Snively Expedition as Told to John S. Ford," *Southwestern Historical Quarterly*, LXX (July, 1966).

Ramsdell, C. W. "The Texas State Military Board, 1862–1865," *Southwestern Historical Quarterly*, XXVII (April, 1924).

Rundell, Walter. "Texas Petroleum History: A Selective Annotated Bibliography," *Southwestern Historical Quarterly*, LXVII (October, 1963).

Sandbo, Anna Irene. "Beginnings of the Secession Movement in

Texas," *Southwestern Historical Quarterly*, XVIII (October, 1914).

———. "First Session of the Secession Convention in Texas," *Southwestern Historical Quarterly*, XVIII (October, 1914).

Shook, Robert W. "The Battle of the Nueces, August 10, 1862," *Southwestern Historical Quarterly*, LXVI (July, 1962).

Smyrl, Frank H. "Texans in the Union Army, 1861–1865," *Southwestern Historical Quarterly*, LXV (October, 1961).

Stafford, James. "Behind the NASA Move to Houston," *Texas Business Review*, XXXVI (April, 1962).

Swenson, Loyd S., Jr. "The Fertile Crescent: the South's Role in the National Space Program," *Southwestern Historical Quarterly*, LXXI (January, 1968).

Trahern, George Washington. "Texas Cowboy from Mier to Buena Vista" (ed. A. Russell Buchanan), *Southwestern Historical Quarterly*, LVIII (July, 1954).

NASA Fact Sheets and Printed Papers

Day, Richard E. *Flight Crew Requirements*. NASA Fact Sheet #133. Houston, 1963.

Dryden, Hugh L. *Impact of Progress in Space on Science: Address at Joint Session of the Federation of American Societies for Experimental Biology, April 16, 1962, Atlantic City, New Jersey.* Houston, 1962.

Emme, Eugene M. *Historical Origins of National Aeronautics and Space Administration.* NASA Fact Sheet #110. Washington, 1962.

Faget, Maxime A. *Engineering and Scientific Goals of the NASA Manned Space Flight Program.* NASA Fact Sheet #125. Houston, 1963.

Gilruth, Robert R. *Interview with Data Magazine.* NASA Fact Sheet #114. Houston, 1962.

Hodge, John D., and Tecywn Roberts. *Flight Operations Facilities.* NASA Fact Sheet #131. Houston, 1963.

Kotanchik, Joseph N., and H. Kurt Strass. *Test Facilities of the Manned Spacecraft Center.* NASA Fact Sheet #126. Houston, 1963.

MSC Constructing Permanent Facilities at Clear Lake. NASA Fact Sheet #60. Houston, 1962.

Project Gemini Fact Sheet. Rev. ed. Houston, 1962.

Purser, Paul E. *Questions and Answers.* Houston, 1961.

———. *The Scope of the NASA Research Laboratory at Clear Lake, Texas.* Houston, 1962.

Seamans, Robert C., Jr. *The National Space Program—Progress and Opportunities: Address Before the Washington Representatives Chapter of the National Security Industrial Association.* NASA Fact Sheet #111. Houston, 1963.

Voas, Robert B. *Astronaut Training.* NASA Fact Sheet #139. Houston, 1963.

Yeater, Elwyn H. *The NASA Spacecraft Center and Its Programs.* NASA Fact Sheet #112. Houston, 1962.

INTERVIEWS

Robert H. Brewer, Houston Chamber of Commerce, Houston, August 2, 1963.

Ben Gillespie, Chief of Industrial Communications Branch, NASA's Manned Spacecraft Center, Houston, July 22, 1963.

James M. Grimwood, Historian of NASA's Manned Spacecraft Center, Houston, July 22, 1963.

Eugene E. Horton, NASA's Manned Spacecraft Center, Houston, July 22, 1963.

John W. McFarland, Superintendent of the Houston Independent School District, Houston, August 2, 1963.

Howard N. Martin, Manager of the Research Department of the Houston Chamber of Commerce, Houston, August 2, 1963.

Paul E. Purser, Special Assistant to the Director of NASA's Manned Spacecraft Center, Houston, July 22, 1963.

Index

The paper on which this book is printed bears the watermark of the University of Oklahoma Press and has an effective life of at least three hundred years.